FIRST
DISCIPLINE
DISCIPLINE OF DISCIPLINES

FIRST
DISCIPLINE
DISCIPLINE OF DISCIPLINES

Re-emergence of Asian Management

JOSEPH MANUEL
WITH
SANKAR RADHAKRISHNAN

PARTRIDGE
A Penguin Random House Company

To order additional copies of this book, contact
Partridge India
000 800 10062 62
www.partridgepublishing.com/india
orders.india@partridgepublishing.com

CONTENTS

FOREWORD

First Discipline (FD) is the discipline of disciplines, the base from which other disciplines are derived. Disciplines—art, science or religion—are but collections of maps of physical or virtual spaces. Literate or illiterate, we cannot survive without maps. We start with models and when the results meet our expectations consistently, we elevate them to the level of maps. An example is the periodic table. At the highest level, maps connect meta-disciplines, unifying them into knowledge and wisdom. The silos get connected; the self is the agent of learning and the transformation of data into information, creating sense, meaning and structure. It follows that FD is also the study of the self in relation to the whole, from the level of the personal to the family, groups, organisations, and society.

Technological bandwidth increases at a frenetic pace. We also find instances of human bandwidth shrinking even faster. This paradox dictates that we develop a framework—a lens—that facilitates analytics and integration, seeing and showing the deep structures to achieve much higher levels of integration

Growth is a process of resolving issues of identity, moving from dependence to independence and to interdependence. Individuals, teams, organisations and communities need to go through the process. Copying from less complex contexts is not enough to stay ahead; it is essential to go far beyond imitation to create competitive advantages. FD offers an analytic and integration tool and methodology to address these challenges and disconnects. Through visual semiotics, it incorporates eco-literacy, the new spirituality of work, system thinking, cultural archetypes, continual renewal, mental maps, personal mastery and other unifiers to work together like an operating system of the self at different levels. Transfer of learning and mastery of competences happen at a faster pace in comparison to any other approach. If the world has turned out to be imperfect, it has more to do with these models of the world than the world outside. The visual semiotic tool, the new eyes, show us a coherent whole, giving us the new vision that is an essential prerequisite to creating a more desirable future. As in the case of a terrestrial journey, the approach incorporates positioning, measurement, feedback and reflection—functions that are carried out by the compass, clock and the feedback system—that enable the traveller to be on course.

How and what we learn as individuals and communities will decide our common future. Targeted learning is context—and problem-specific and seeks to connect, reflect and catalyse, better, faster and deeper. The pace of learning is the differentiator in the race for market share. Technology and the Internet have changed the paradigms of learning. The full impact is not felt since habits linger. It is feasible now to leave rote learning to memory devices, freeing time and effort for more productive purposes. Learning on a need to learn basis at the time it is required is feasible. The self mediates in the process of transformation of data into information and knowledge, creating sense, meaning and structure, in turn leading to learning and improvement. Mastery of this process, at the level of individuals, organisations, community and society at large is critical for the developmental process.

Icons and symbols, like road signs and traffic signals, can function like a compass. The Graphic User Interface accelerated the emergence of a connected world. Within the networks is silicon, which has the innate quality of connecting and forming very long chains. Digital and other deeper disconnects of multiple dimensions slow down the journey towards the higher evolutionary potential—individual or collective—in us, creating serious threats to the very survival of the species. Marshall Goldsmith tells us *What Got You Here Won't Get You There*. If we go by history and precedence, we wouldn't have made the moon shots. History is created when we make it history.

The nature of the common journey is that we move towards our completeness and to greater completeness. A parallel can be drawn for this journey too, similar to our other journeys. Let us say that the journey begins now and that the direction is fixed. We are in Bangalore and the time is 10 am on 31 May 2013. We would like to go to Mumbai. As we take every step on our journey to Mumbai, we need to make sure that we are moving in the right direction and not away from it. We need a compass/map and the clock to do this. This is reflecting, looking back and forth to make sure that the process is on track. The three keywords are Position, Direction and Reflection—the essentials to take on the physical world. Given the other requisites, one is certain to reach Mumbai. Without the first three, all the rest will not take us to Mumbai.

Mapping the physical world has become very precise in our times. Between Galileo's telescope, the Hubble and the Femtoscope, are the very large and the very small—farther and deeper. The observer connects the two, attempting to comprehend the whole. Yet we will never comprehend the whole in its totality. At best it will always remain an approximation and there will always be unknowables. What we can comprehend of the physical world is so vast that a system is required to navigate it.

The journey of life is much more than a journey through external space since we are much more than our physical selves. How does one position oneself for this journey? It is the self which fixes the position, direction and reflects on itself as to the progress of the process. The observer and the observed are parts of the same system. Mapping the whole system, physical, nonphysical, external and internal and evolving a navigational tool is one of the basic requisites for the journey on that less travelled road.

From 1981 to 1990, we worked towards evolving the First Discipline Framework (FDF), the road map. Eco-literacy, the new spirituality, system thinking, cultural archetypes, continual renewal, mental maps, personal mastery and many more unifiers are embedded in the tool. Since then, we have used the tool for dialogue in diverse contexts, though dialogue is not in our habit. Politicians and priests preach, professionals prescribe, teachers lecture, parents advise. Dialogue needs adults, not leaders and followers or shepherds and sheep. The approach is process—and dialogue-based, in real time, stretching without burnout and improves alignment at deeper levels of the self for sustained high performance. Dream work, re-framing of mental maps through storytelling/writing, envisioning and action learning in a simulated work environment are some aspects of the methodology. The context and details vary, but the principles remain the same. Since going online from May 2008, the dialogue continues globally and in real time.

This living document is the outcome of this continual dialogue. It gets written on its own. Over the years, several thousands—a majority of them from the edges—have participated in the process. I/we in the document represent any one or the community which includes me. Among others, I remain one of the facilitators to the process and I alone am responsible for the biases, errors, omissions and jargon that possibly have crept in.

There are many dots to be connected; welcome to the dialogue and to connecting more of them.

Joseph Manuel

CHAPTER 1

On design, dialogue, development, community and communication for capacity-building for livelihood/ food security

The dialogue

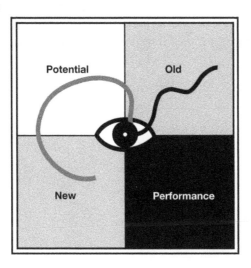

"A new scientific truth does not triumph by convincing its opponents and making them see the light, but rather because its opponents eventually die, and a new generation grows up that is familiar with it."—Max Planck

Spinoza (1632-1677) was a lens maker. Lenses correct visual aberrations. Their use in microscopes and telescopes gives us both far and in-depth views of reality. He had the rarest of rare inner lenses to 'see' beyond the obvious making him immortal despite his short life. Did he 'see' what he was doing to himself? Do we 'see' where the 'Pipers of Hamlin' are taking us?

- What we see is what we get. A broken lens gives us a broken view.
- An unbroken view is an imperative for sustainability (anti-fragility?).
- Multiple views are essential to 'see' through the heights of complexity.
- What is excluded in the act of seeing might be even more significant than what is 'seen'.

This book points to where we are designed to go. The non-linear, spiral-like road in the visual at the beginning of this chapter takes us to growth, continual renewal and the evolutionary potential of the species. The relatively linear path in the top right quadrant takes us to traffic blocks, accidents and death. Technology helps us reach there faster, on massive scales. Does it make a difference to arrive in a Ferrari or on foot? To make the correct choice we need to be mature, curious and have information. Chances are extremely slim that we 'see' the significance of design. Are we programmed to fail? Is the child in us stolen? We live in the age of WMD, weapons of Mass Dialogue/ Destruction. This dialogue, though, is about the travellers' kit—how to assemble, re-assemble oneself to travel on the path of perfection.

The road most travelled or not travelled, we are free to choose.

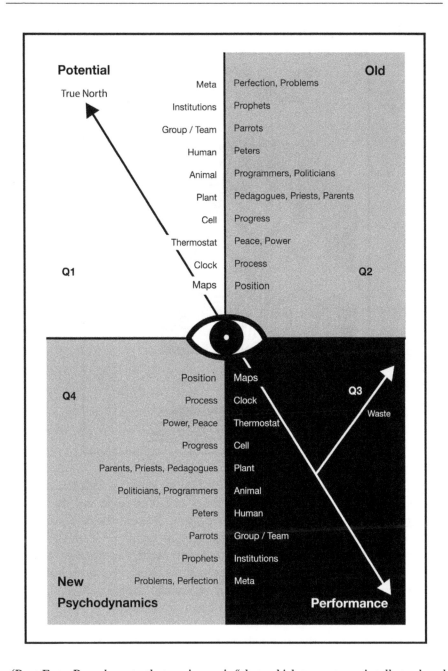

(Poet Ezra Pound wrote that an image is "that which presents an intellectual and emotional complex in an instant of time". Pound goes on to state "It is better to present one image in a lifetime than to produce voluminous works.")

Slumdog billions, an ecosystem view

The miniature ecosystem (see graphic) has an eagle, a vulture, a small community of frogs, a tree and a very deep well. The eagle and the vulture come to perch on the tree. The frogs have always lived in the deep well from which they have never gone out, nor can they move out of it on their own; they only dream of the external world. Every night, the granny frog tells bedtime stories to the young ones in the well. Most of the stories have been passed down over generations with an occasional improvisation here and there. The eagle and the vulture at times listen to the stories.

One morning, when the thermals had begun rising in the air, the eagle swoops down into the well, grasps one little frog in its claws and rises up with the thermals. The heights and the fear of death grip the little one. The eagle stays with the thermal, circling over the well and when it finds that the little one has calmed down a little, it releases the frog from its claws. The vulture waits in the hope that the frog will turn carrion. The frog lands back in the same well, unhurt, still afraid and probably elated. During the free ride the frog had opened its eyes for a brief moment to get a glimpse of the world outside the well. The eagle returns to the tree waiting for the sun to set, to hear the new stories.

The Oscars, The curious case of Benjamin Button and the Slumdog Millionaire

The *Slumdog Millionaire* swept the first Oscars since the recession of 2008. It is perhaps more than coincidental that we dream up another version of the rags to riches story when billions vanish in the stock market and the market caps reach rock bottom. There is no greater fantasy than to beat a recession when the 'developed world' reels in its flames. 'Developed', stands for the 'top of the pyramid' within the context of the book, with no geopolitical connotations.

The children from Dharavi, the Bombay (Mumbai) slum, who were part of the film flew up to Oscar heights, shedding their slum maps of the world for the eagle's view from the top; at least for a fleeting moment. Or was it the vulture's view? When they returned, the well would still be the same. Yet some things will never be the same. For fleeting moments, the bottom and the top connect and the media goes into overdrive vying with each other to generate our daily dose of adrenaline.

The slum dogs and the dogs in Beverly Hills/ Malabar Hill, have the same DNA, the same potential. So does the human. Other than the cosmetic, the dog's potential is not far behind in terms of its performance. It is still a dog's life. Some might quarrel for morsels while the lucky ones, the adopted ones, don't have to. Research shows us they give up some of their intelligence. Domesticated dogs are less intelligent than the stray ones. The story of the human is not the same. We could be much better than the dogs, wherever they are. The bottom and the top of the pyramid are connected through fantasy and fiction.

We need a design to make this leap-frogging happen on a regular, continual basis. Mobility accelerates learning. Dreams, celluloid or lucid, connect better to our deep structures and at times can help us awaken into a better future.

In 2008, 290,000 candidates appeared for CAT, the common admission test to the Indian Institutes of Management. The process is not very different from the Dharavi kid turning into the slumdog millionaire, though the chances are less than 0.6%. Another 100,000 will join US universities to pursue their dreams of flight. Some of them will join the Million Dollar league and work towards reaching the top of the pyramid. Others will trail behind and wrack their brains on how to beat them in the race. A few of them would turn entrepreneurial or find other ways to win their millions. Some will completely opt out of the race to move to the bottom of the pyramid. Bose, an IIM batch mate who opted out of the race to the top, tells me that b-school days still bring back memories of street dogs fighting for their morsels; Pavlov's dogs for whom the bell tolls. The CEO of a bank walks away with a lifetime pension of over £650,000/annum leaving the ship he was captaining to sink, a typical role model for the participants of the race. But things do change overnight; during the slowdown governance was back in fashion.

Around 30,000 Indians—people who successfully chased similar dreams—return from the US every year to settle down in their home country for various reasons. The story is a much better version than Danny Boyle coming down to Dharavi. Within an individual lifespan, a critical mass of people have flown out of their individual wells, fulfilled their dreams and will return to the same well. The well has not changed much, but many of them see new possibilities in leapfrogging at a larger scale, bringing together the best of both worlds. Twenty-seven per cent of the world's poor are in India. If the bottom suffers from abject poverty, the top suffers from intellectual poverty; two sides of the same coin. The challenge is to see the third side—the side/s that connect the two. The farmer who feeds the bottom and the top hopes and prays for the monsoons to continue to be favourable, that the government increases the procurement prices and that loans be written off. As in the case of the bailout billions, the relatively non-performing among them are more likely to end up receiving such relief. Perhaps in an election year, the procurement prices will be higher than the cost, inclusive of the share of the rats and vultures in the ecosystem.

Climbing Mount Everest (Hillary and Tensing), the Wright brothers and flight, the moon shot—in short every human achievement has a common thread that connects to the whole. At one end of the continuum is the well, the local, and at the other is the very large, the global. To learn is to connect the two, a bolt of lightning from the blue connecting both.

Once we take the invariant position that we are here to learn and learn continually, then it is a journey of connecting the small with the large, the local with the global. What we see changes with the variant positions we take during the journey. Something new comes into our perspective, improving the old maps. Development is a process of connecting potential to performance and narrowing the gap between the two. The eagle/frog frames are joined together to produce the movie of our individual lives. Whether we direct it on our own or get directed is what matters most! If we learn the lessons right and shed our preoccupations with the maps of change and quantitative growth over quality, we could leverage it to come out of recessions and booms and busts to a phase of continual improvement in the quality of life, community and sustainability.

C. K. Prahlad reinvented the pyramid for our time—the realisation that there is a fortune at the bottom of the pyramid! It has always been a trend with the top of the pyramid to come down to the bottom in search of the treasures for different reasons. Warren Buffet and Bill Gates connect to connect to the bottom. We hear academics wondering now, a bit too late perhaps, is business ANTI social so that wealth needs to be balanced with charity? What does charity beget? The circle is now complete! Until creation of wealth and business turns pro-community, charity seems to be the dominant paradigm by which we connect to the bottom; the current version of the missionary zeal of the colonial era. Some of them were in for a surprise and those who connected in a spirit of learning to the bottom brought to light many a treasure. Mohammed Yunus in Bangladesh and the White Revolution in India pointed to the directions in beating a recession.

The moral is more important than the story. One has to be a frog at times and an eagle at others, and keep switching positions continually to connect between the local and the global. With every leap of the frog there is a collapse of an old world and a new world takes birth. Yet we are in the same well, the well of Nature, which we will never fully comprehend. It might make us a little more humble and help us realise that we cannot reinvent the basic design. Meanwhile, there is a lull; no thermals seem to be in the making to those who reel in the flames of the recession. The vultures wait for the feast. The thermals are always in the making, some place or the other.

The original story of *The Curious Case of Benjamin Button* was published in 1921, the same year that Albert Einstein received the Nobel Prize. We cannot age backwards like the protagonist of the story and meet Scott Fitzgerald to find out why he wrote the story or whether he agrees with the film adaptation of the story, which begins with a curious clock maker, which goes well with the overall theme. Let us also hope that he wouldn't object to colouring the story to suit our present context. The extreme geriatric, the process of his aging backwards and the curious clock that goes back in time triggers one to reflect on our present reality. The clock is a simple machine without self-regulation. The technology that we have developed remains mostly at this level of maturity. While we are no doubt scaling the ladder to higher levels of technology with increasing self-regulation, as a culture we are no better than the clock, a metaphor for the Newtonian world view. Extreme geriatrics has come to be our collective illness. Benjamin Button is turned out of Yale because he ran out of the cosmetics he used to hide his age. The gates of knowledge were closed to him though later on, when he grows younger, he makes a second attempt to make it to Harvard but fails to graduate as he loses his learn-ability to the pace of his growing young.

The *Origin of Species by Means of Natural Selection or the Preservation of Favoured Races in the Struggle for Life* was first published in 1859. We have three different sets of maps but we fail to connect these maps together and evolve a common one. Charles Darwin was way ahead of Isaac Newton and Einstein in dealing with emergent qualities between classes of life. Even to the untrained eye, these qualities are discernible—that no machines come anywhere near a cell, that from the unicellular to the multi-cellular is a giant leap and within the multi-cellular, plants, animals, human and community have higher levels of complexity and potential that the lower levels do not possess. Still, our collective reality has not moved ahead from the level of the clock. Even 150 years after the publication of the *Origin of Species*, the essential learning remains outside our collective understanding of reality and makes us a less favoured species in the struggle for survival.

The Curious Case of Benjamin Button captures all the limitations of the Newtonian paradigm. While humanity moves ahead on the path of decay and ageing to self-destruction, the hero goes against the flow; but the ultimate destiny is not altered. Cosmetic solutions will not gain us admittance to understanding, but they contribute significantly to the bubbles and busts. Real learning would help us design real solutions. Between the positive and negative flows of time is emergence, the bolt from the blue that negates entropy and decay. Accumulating real learning helps us beat the fate of the tragic hero *The Curious Case of Benjamin Button* proved predictive, prophetic, of our current reality. Conflict is part of the story of evolution. We have reached the apex of the pyramid of conflicts. Yet another emergence is in the offing.

Design, development, community and communication for capacity-building for livelihood / food security

Kerala in South India on the 12 N parallel, is a hot spot for tourists and test marketers. With 28 times the density of population of the US, 1/70th GDP per capita and a comparable quality of life on many indicators of human development as that of the US, the state is a paradox for the social scientist (including Amartya Sen and his less popular detractors).

Kerala has a much shorter history of freedom than the US and nothing great to boast of in leadership or quality of governance. Leadership and quality of governance in Kerala are much like the couple in a troubled marriage between the beast and beauty. In their early stages of infatuation and hormonal overdrive they come to have a brood of children. As the infatuation wanes, the decibel levels climb to new heights of leadership claims from the beast. Beauty succumbs to helpless silence, dreams and prays that the children take to the path of resilience and creativity. Sometimes, her prayers are answered reinforcing her faith in gods, god men and god women. These exceptions, which flourish, are significant enough to ensure that Kerala's people are better off than those in many other developed and developing contexts. Enough of these free radicals are left within the state to ensure that governance alternates every five years between the two loose coalitions. The remaining mass is more or less evenly split between the two factions, addicted in varying degrees to religion or revolution, spirit or spirituality, the lottery and the mafia. Equal opportunities to share the spoils of power ensure that the good or bad that has been achieved by one is undone by the other. Thus, the context has remained fertile for discovering the path to early adulthood, resilience and creativity of a significant few to chase their dreams outside the state. The affliction seems to be spreading to the rest of the country and in more ways than one, Kerala is a beacon to where India is heading—a slow painful path to adulthood of the masses, a bottom-up approach to leaderless development. This is where India scores in competitive advantage over other countries: diversity and chaos fostering creativity and resilience?

Over the two-month period from mid-November to mid-January around fifty million people visit Sabarimala in Kerala's Pathanamthitta district, perhaps making it the largest and most visited annual pilgrimage centre in the world. An Ayappa temple is located here, amidst 18 hills (of the Western Ghats) each of which has a minor temple. Men of all ages and women other than those in the age group of 10 to 50 traverse forest paths to the temple and climb 18 steps for the darshan. Some explain that the ritual is symbolic of the progress through 18 levels to the heights of awareness to arrive where there is no separation between the worshipper and the worshipped. There is no other at this level. Thou art that. Awareness and conscious evolution is a well-defined path to the supreme for which they prepare themselves through an elaborate process often lasting up to forty days.

Indian myths hold that there are fourteen worlds in all, seven over and seven under. In another myth integral to every Keralite's software, Vamana, an avatar of Vishnu, traverses all the fourteen worlds in just two steps. Mahabali, the Asura king offers his own head for the third step to keep his word to the avatar in disguise. The myth about the transformational journey from the personal to the cosmic self can be translated into the visual for easier understanding of the process.

Three steps are imperatives for any journey in space, improvement or developmental process:

1. Finding one's starting position; the compass /GPS function.

2. Choosing the direction/evolving a map for the journey.

3. Reflecting, making sure that progress is real; the process of comparing and measuring the present position with the home position and where one ought to be.

Mapping (design), measurement (clock), and informed decisions (thermostat) are integral to the use of tools (technology). Mastery of the inanimate world is the prelude to mastery of the animate, beginning with the world of the unicellular. The cell is a symbolic representative of this class. The three imperatives are programmed, natural to the cell, integral to its natural intelligence, making it a class apart from the levels preceding it.

The cell is true to its design. It delivers what it is designed to perform, which is to state that it performs perfectly. If only the systems we design have this level of perfection. For example the Dreamliner has a reliability of above 0.9 and the moon missions 0.98. The cell has a reliability of 1. Now we know where we stand in terms of perfection. We now have the rough framework for a practice of the first of the six levels of perfection.

The second practice of perfection follows from the world of plants, a much higher level of complexity and variety than that of the cell. Every plant is rooted and reaches out towards the sun, connecting the local with the global. We cannot improve on the design of the ecosystem nor do we have reason to complain other than our failure to connect to the imperatives that follow from design in nature so that our designs move in the direction of perfection.

The practice of six perfections corresponds to six different levels of increasing variety, complexity and potential. Each level triggers questions as to the outcomes of the practice. The Dreamliner and the moon missions are systems designed by the human who, at the individual level, has a reliability of 0. It is human to err! It is inhuman for the human to err. The cell, plants and animals are perfect. It is also human to aspire for perfection, pursue truth and beauty. The human is perfect in design, but the practice flounders. Maturity is not achieved overnight for a system that takes over two decades to physically mature.

Some illustrative questions that trigger the practice of perfections at each of the levels are:

1. That of the cell: Am I at least as intelligent as a single cell, such as an amoeba or a single cell in my body, in self-regulation?

2. That of the plant: Am I rooted, connected to my own past, culture and community so that I can take position and reach out towards freedom and growth?

3. That of the animal: Why is it that the animal is never obese, never visits the shrink, doesn't have annual physicals (not applicable to our pets) or make social calls to friends in hospitals?

4. That of the human: Why are we the only species that generates waste? Why are we the only class of beings with the lowest capacity utilisation factor? With a reliability of 0, is free will a myth?

5. That of the organisation: Are businesses inherently anti-social, and therefore need to have a separate agenda for CSR?

6. That of community: How to practice design and delivery of solutions/products/services that meet real outcomes of sustainability and enhanced community?

For the naturalist there is only nature and no 'supernature'. By the same logic, there is no premium on virtual reality over reality, artificial intelligence over intelligence, virtual sex over real sex or the masculine over the feminine. The substitutes for the real have come to threaten the very survival of the species and one wonders whether the species is committing mass suicide, madly rushing towards its own destruction in the search for substitutes to a harsh reality.

From the tree to the woods and the forest

The best teachers do the least teaching and the best leaders the least leading. They SEE where we are and point their fingers to SHOW us the direction we ought to take. Over three decades ago, we were taught by two of the best teachers that I have come across. They asked us to self-teach an introductory course on Management Information Systems and Computers. It fell on me to introduce the class to Kenneth Boulding, 'General systems theory: The skeleton of science'.

The skeleton in the cupboard took on flesh and blood over the years. The desktops were yet to show up, the mainframe was a remote presence which one tried to visualise through programming sheets and punched cards. Later on when the desktops appeared, the black box with the blinking C prompt beckoned one to navigate the hidden pathways. The management theory jungle was in no way different from the black box of the desktops. Imagine the plight of a novice to the profession mired in the semantic swamp being confronted with a still higher complexity of the market place against the compulsions of meeting targets and deadlines by the end of the next quarter! Worse still, being in academics at the time; how do you communicate Boulding to an audience of senior managers attending their very first introductory session on management, and do it in 60 minutes?

Remember they also introduced you to innovation. How do you communicate to those who call the shots (whether to retain you or fire you) or to a larger group hardwired to their own disciplines who act as the agents for a population of over a million on the edges of society in every sense of the term and make an impact. Big data and an Ivy League stamp won't do. One has to show and to show one has to SEE.

Many views, one reality

If India offers the heights of complexity, the eco-system people are at the peak, the Everest of complexity. The tribal is already edged out from their commons. The artisanal fishermen linger on primarily because the 'law of the sea' remains incomprehensible to those immersed in the 'law of the land'. We seldom realise that marginalising them is nothing short of suicidal, a failure to SEE the connections.

Making of the lens/The meta-systems view/Design of the learning engine

The meta-analytic framework

13

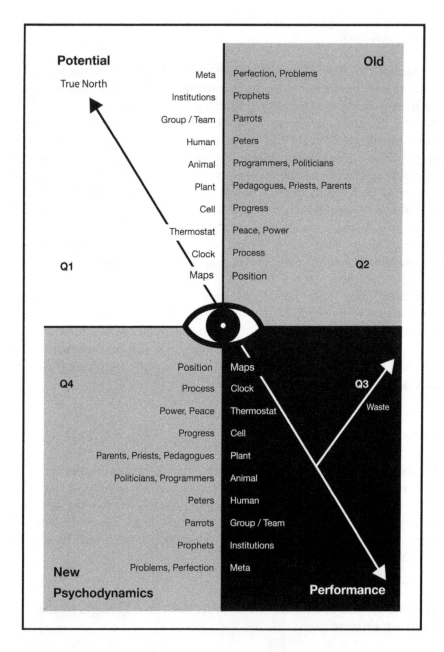

(We are the only species which generates waste. We don't think it is intentional. It is only because we don't SEE the connections. Improvement is reduction in waste. If we apply the human analogy, for every standing tree, a 1/2 trillion of pollen would have gone to waste. Is this waste or design? The same logic applied

to seven billion living humans tells us that a handful would suffice to fulfil the evolutionary requirement of survival of the species. At true north, there is zero waste. We now have a universal non-controversial reference point, a basis for community, around which regardless of personal belief systems, people could come together. We could also SHOW the gap between where we are now to where we ought to be across the diversity of contexts.)

Spinoza, who we met earlier in this chapter, was both a lens maker and a philosophers' philosopher. While he had the rarest lens to SEE far beyond his time, making him immortal, perhaps he failed to SEE what he was doing to himself. The very act of seeing excludes something else which may be even more significant. Invariably our internal lenses are at fault for what we SEE. These visual aberrations need correction to design sustainable solutions. A combination of lenses and multiple views become necessary to SEE through the heights of complexity. Boulding had proposed the framework to bring together all possible lenses from diverse disciplines. We just had to deal with the user interface challenge with a few add-ons to accommodate the imperatives of managerial performance. The process took nine years and many near-deaths, but something very tangible could now be delivered in those 60 minutes.

In the visual of the First Discipline Framework above, Q 1 is a visual representation of what Boulding SAW as the skeleton of science, and Q3 the mirror opposite, the concrete tangible world. The gap between potential and performance in any system can now be visualised. Q3 and Q4 explains the why and how of the gap. Fitting in specific data sets to specific contexts is no big deal. Showing that we are caught up between our own past and the future is achieved in no time, the pre-requisite to transcending the blocks. The gap is bridged without any resistance because it is in our own interest to improve. The blue oceans become visible, navigation is easier and the distant shores become a tangible reality. The only facilitation is an initiation to see the knowledge holes. Solutions emerge naturally. Tested at varying levels of complexity the framework holds well across levels and contexts. Learning faster than the competition is the only real competitive advantage. Sustainable performance follows when the learning engine—individuals, institutions, communities—continually improves on its previous best performance.

Indeed a picture is worth a forest equivalent of paper consumed by discussions on contra causal free will!

Complexity is addictive when one is fascinated by elegant solutions. Having arrived at one, one is tempted to use it like the proverbial Maslow's hammer: "I suppose it is tempting, if the only tool you have is a hammer, to treat everything as if it were a nail." Every context is unique and the introduction of a new hammer influences the context more often in a contra-causal manner, good intentions creating the opposite impact. The hammer has to be judged against tangible outcomes where appropriate metrics come to substantiate the tools.

Focus: Climbing Everest first, the waves and the poor rich

With the mastery of lens making we can focus Femtoscopes/Hubbles—the vision compass—to where we want to pay our attention. If you are a mountain climber, Everest is the gold standard of climbing. The Indian side offers a much higher level of complexity than the Chinese because of the diversity of languages, colour, religion, politics and so on. The ecosystem people are at the extreme edge of this complexity in every sense of the term. It was among the artisanal fishing community of Kerala that we focused our vision compass. The solutions were to be evolved in a participatory mode. There was no escape from getting wet to learn swimming and fishing.

The ecosystem people have or had shared, free and open access to their commons, the forests and water bodies, just as we have Wiki now. The forest dweller and the artisanal fishermen are in reality the custodians of our common future though they have been edged out of their commons by us, their 'civilised' tech and market savvy cousins. Their livelihoods are threatened because we fail to see that our common future is at stake. The farmers' plight is much less complex in comparison. Livelihoods, food and water security are but different views of the same reality. For now, we will focus on the artisanal fishermen leaving the farmer and the forest dweller for later discussions.

Big data, finding directions at sea

We had volumes and volumes of data. The Indian Institute of Management (Ahmedabad) had carried out a benchmark study, running into several volumes, of the fisheries sector of India. There were international agencies like the FAO to turn to. But how do you know where to focus the search and how do we make sense of big data to decide our position as a prelude to fixing the direction to move in. The directions were to be shown to a community of over a million people often qualified as the poorest of the poor, illiterate.

Sometimes solutions surface from the most unexpected corners.

We were working with the MSY (maximum sustainable yield) estimates and annual landing figures for fish to optimise fishing effort and returns to the community and prioritise intervention points. It was the second day of a three-day marathon workshop when one of the participants mustered up her courage and talked about her previous night's dream.

She said, "It is not a straight line, it is a wave" and went on to explain with the help of a diagram that what she said was just another version of the dream that Joseph had to interpret for the Pharaoh.

It made immense sense to all. It is all about waves on the sea or the markets. The MSY is a wave, so are the landings across the long—and short terms, the financial flows move in the opposite direction to the physical flows, there are good years and bad years and years when there are higher risks of over-exploitation. There is a definite pattern. Vessels have anchors and the community needed anchors of stability to withstand the clash of the waves in production from the markets and the clash of different cultures, the most fundamental of which is a clash between the logic of the land and the sea.

We could now translate the vision to a business development plan and reduce the complexity of operations to a few spreadsheets. Goodbye, big data.

The vision compass could be turned to other contexts

Yet another view: The community learning engine

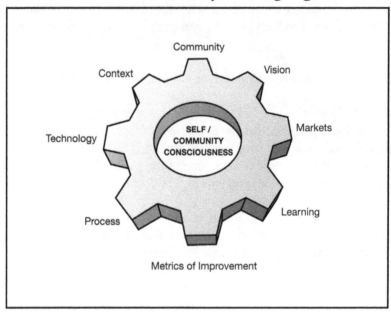

Technology and markets are two major levers to bring about improvement. Some communities have achieved remarkable progress is using them. But conventional measures of improvement fail to grasp the cost at which such improvements are achieved. Economic growth needs to be balanced with improvement in community. Some communities have achieved physical quality of life at a much lower cost to the community and there are also communities like the ecosystem people where in spite of improvements in growth, corresponding improvements in quality of life have not materialised. The focus here is on how a particular community responds to the challenges of managing technology and markets along with improvement in community.

Old wine, new bottles

It took us more time to realise that the design of the learning engine was nothing but very old wine in a new bottle, a modern version of Nagarjuna's inference engine, the wheel of dharma and many other similar representations. The Greeks had their 'tetra-lemma' the equivalent of 'Catushkodi' in the east. Ashoka and Alexander, Buddha and Christ were realisations of this higher vision of that age of reason spread across a golden period of global community that lasted for a few centuries. The bell rings from Sarnath, the lion capital of Ashoka. 'Sar' in Sanskrit means the essence and 'nath' means sound. On top of the bell are the four lions, back to back, representing the four visions that help us anchor to the centre and the middle-path? Ashoka pillars were erected all over his empire and the chakra found its way to the national flag of the country. Ashoka knew that visual literacy was important to hold the empire together. Once again, the visual is taking over, throwing up the possibility of mass dialogue, development and transformation at a pace and scale unprecedented in history.

Suggested reading

Can Asians Think?—Kishore Mahbubani

The End of the Nation State—Kenichi Ohmae

On Dialogue, Culture, and Organisational Learning—Edgar H. Schein

Charles Eames' Quotes:

"Eventually, everything connects—people, ideas, objects . . . the quality of the connections is the key to quality per se."

"Beyond the age of information is the age of choices."

"I don't believe in this 'gifted few' concept, just in people doing things they are really interested in doing. They have a way of getting good at whatever it is."

CHAPTER 2

New Literacy

The Dawkins delusion

Dawkins Delusion
Rhymes well
No better reason
A leadership delusion
Driven by what he attempts to debunk
That some are born to lead, explain
Show the way, we are the sheep
Psychopaths, wolves in sheep's clothing
If we were adults, we wouldn't be led
Information would rule the world
Horses would have wings
Dawkins and Haw Kings wouldn't ride
Admit a few things unexplainable
That makes it worth getting up in the morn
Dawkins and Haw Kings wouldn't sell
If they spare a Spinoza or Einstein
That's where they would love to be
Saints in the church of reason
Galileo is in Da Vinci is out
In their court of inquisition
Too crowded for art and the mystic
The world is flat, hot and crowded
And we are fried
The twain shall never meet
Let the parrots flourish, and
Thank God, we have an economy
Don't kamplain
Says the New Inglish Dictionary
Top of Form

Any thoughts?
On the therapeutics of FB
Don't hear the shrinks kamplain
Of the palace of delusions

"The purpose of science is not to cure us of our sense of mystery and wonder," Stanford's Robert Sapolsky famously noted, "but to constantly reinvent and reinvigorate it."

The piper of Hamlin

Do you hear the music?

Seductive 'ringing little bells'

Day and night

He is singing for the rats

Rat-singer

Pay him his due

"Render unto Caesar the things which are Caesar's,

And unto God the things that are God's"

Else he will sing

The child in you will be stolen

None left to say "The Emperor is naked"

The doors remain barred, for

"Truly I tell you, unless you change and become like little children

You will never enter the kingdom of heaven."

Infographic thinking

Maps are not the territory. But without maps we are unable to deal with territory. Imagine thinking of the planet before the space missions. The process that we document here began in 1980 when some of us took our invariant position as Facilitators. The visual that follows is a map of this journey that we have taken and share with those who joined us on the way. The text assumes meaning only in relation to this map.

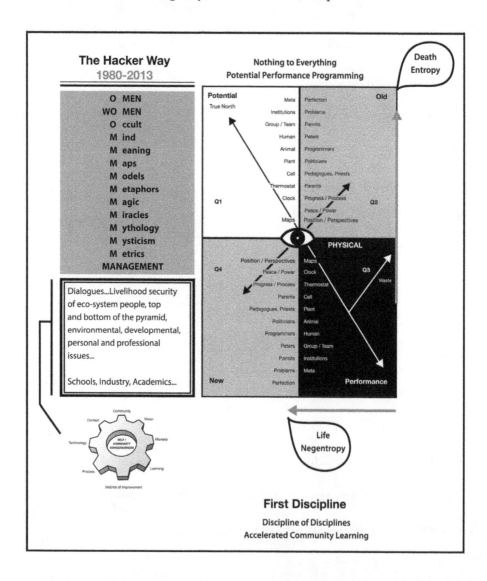

Text is used as a means to create an internal image like in the earlier verse on the Piper of Hamlin; to create a map we need to learn to learn all over again—be like little children.

You may be a PhD but you are illiterate!

In 1981, my painter friend Rob shocked me with the statement above. To him, I must have come across as one of those arrogant MBA types. He tested me with a few simple questions and proved to me that I was visually illiterate.

Later on, I came to recognise that I am illiterate in many other modes too. Post Wall Street, Rob would have framed the question differently:

"You may be a Wharton (or some such) MBA, but you are illiterate."

So what were those questions?

Making them public would destroy the mystique that I have created around my IP—intellectual property/poverty depending on the positions we take. I have sent a whisper note; if you don't grasp it you may be illiterate on some other scale.

People should not be unsettled from their comfort zones. It might do them good but it could spoil your reputation. So I play the diplomat, but diplomacy came to me after many hard knocks over three decades.

"But I am a PhD," responds Dr Nazki over FB. I first met him in 1976. We re-connected on FB a few years back.

He is a black swan, a retired professor of veterinary science; but not tired. Yes, a PhD, but better and more widely known for his literary pursuits. I believe poets and painters are literate in a very different way. In an earlier era they would prefer to be in Paris than in the company of the likes of me. Dr Nazki was the first multimodal person I met. Thanks to him I was already prepared in some way to learn from the shocker from Rob.

Thanks to social media, I can continue in my well (without going to Paris where I would be even more illiterate) and yet remain in touch—at a distance—without being a victim of the porcupine logic.

Most learning happens at the edges

Farmers and fishermen are insulated from each other by different versions of literacy. There is a perception of stability on land, but very little on the high seas. Fisherwomen are not as insulated as men. When mobile phones came on the scene, the illiterate fishermen were ahead of their literate agent in getting them. Vasco da Gama was more literate than Columbus. He reached where he wanted to go.

Literacy has to be judged against the outcomes

Edges go beyond the geographic. There exists a divide between the biologist and the physicist as with the farmer and the fisherman, poets and painters and the fictional average goose. Newton continues to influence the metaphors and paradigms of the literate much more than Einstein or Darwin. *The Trouble with Physics* (Lee Smolin) or cosmology is that the proponents are illiterate about biology. Physics is more in fashion than biology. Both perhaps are illiterate about the lens with which we see the world. We are not talking about seer scientists like Einstein who come closer to poets and painters who are more in alignment with their deeper selves.

Literacy, in a traditional sense, is the ability to manipulate symbols and make sense; in other words, read, write and think critically. I wish it had been read, write and reflect. Literacy is often equated with modernity and culture. In the beginning was the word and now that we are nearing the end of the word as we knew it, will we turn out to be more literate in the non-traditional sense of the term. The printing press and the East India Company are often perceived as landmarks of the beginning of the 'modern age'. The oral traditions which relied on memory gave in to technology and to those who could leverage technology. The digital frees up much more memory and opens up space for creative endeavour, which could also lead to a void taken over by digital noise in no time. Closed is even better than open at times!

So what is the literacy that we are talking about? I was delighted to see the issues discussed in a classic academic sense by Carey Jewitt of the University of London's London Knowledge Lab in *Multimodality and Literacy in School Classrooms*. I shared this link with the tribe, but there were no takers. Contagiousness is king, rather than content. I would have learnt something if I had some feedback; my experiment in community learning and participatory writing would have paid off. For my tired senior eyes the article was not multimodal. I played Hitler for a while and forced my children and a few members of the tribe to take serious note of the article. They appreciated it, but I had to face questions as to why academic writing cannot be simpler sans the mystique. But for my tryst with illiteracy about livelihood security among the top of the pyramid I would not have played Hitler. Meanwhile Carey writes to us, participatory is working. Sankar mails, pointing to some related issues in a post—The slow life—on his blog Not Too Random. Aby and Sarah comment. I only have to report the process, the output is combinatorial.

What we already know is the blinder to further knowledge. The belief that we are conscious is the worst barrier to our consciousness. (We don't know who said this)

What if there are faster more efficient and effective ways of direct knowing, addressing multiple triggers simultaneously?

In a world that visually unfolds in real time, how long can plain linear static texts compete with much higher bandwidths?

If you are a champion of text, you would do well to migrate to Indian universities where they lament about employability. And the very same people who create the problem are entrusted with the responsibility of solving the issue. The digital divide results in no small measure from the preference for viewing rather than manipulating text. If both sides appear to be morons to each other, do not be surprised.

There is more to the argument that the more literate we are in the traditional sense, the less literate we are from a developmental perspective.

New literacy is about making sense and meaning of the world around us, physical or virtual; reducing the complexity of cues, symbols and noise which facilitates navigation rather than wandering around without purpose or speeding up without knowing where we are heading.

Sankar sends me a link on slowing down—'The joy of quiet by' Pico Iyer. Amitabh shares the same on FB. We have a conversation as to why we should or not slow down. As if by synchronicity I receive a mail from Aphoristic Cocktail: "Nature never hurries, yet all is accomplished."—Lau Tzu

Nature is 'over' designed to be perfect. We work by default, not by design. Rahul asks what is your default setting? We are the only species that comes with the default setting to fail, self-destruct. To be literate is to realise this. When the pace is too fast one fails to see what happens around us. It is all a blur. Slowing down has no intrinsic value unless the slow down helps us see what happens around us. The farmer is slow, but the fishermen cannot afford to be slow. Not all farmers see and not all fishermen are fast enough.

There are craftsmen writers and scientists for whom writing/science is a career and seer scientists like Einstein who thought about relativity for ten years and the special theory of relativity for another ten years. The attention span of the career scientist could be limited by the next paper to be pushed out if he has to stay in circulation.

Read The Trouble with Physics for more and better

We have mastered navigating the physical world. The maps are near perfect though the means could be improved. The virtual remains to be mastered. More often, it is noise and the ability to make noise that prevails. Captain Sparrow with the broken compass is an apt metaphor of our times. Even pirates have their code. "The code wins arguments," silence is restored. Managers are yet to develop one.

Adult education is a mockery of education, proof that the long years of 'educating ourselves' in schools and universities don't turn us into ADULTs, teach us to self-manage instead of mass produce a new version of slavery which certainly appeals to born again Hitlers!

Lifehacking was not coined back then

Nazki the poet, Rob the painter and Professor P.C. Devassia, Indian Sanskrit scholar and poet, were our touchstones for deciphering the literacy code. I met PCD in 1981, when he was 75. He passed away in 2006 at over 100 years fulfilling all the goals that he had declared for himself when he was 60. He could see for forty years.

Passing the lie detector is no proof of truth and truth detectors are not yet in the market. Time will prove whether all the noise has any substance. Has literacy, the real stuff, got anything to do with longevity or sustained high performance? Wiki has a 'list of lists' of centenarians, which comes close to our population of literate people. There are 19 categories in this list of lists.

There is no exclusive list for economists, physicists or physicians. Their theories do not help themselves. Poets, painters, musicians, mathematicians and businessmen appear to be more literate.

The literacy matrix

Smoking causes cancer. Yet, most of the cancer cases around me are people who have never smoked, from families with no history of smoking. Smoking can at best be just one of the many factors that would have gone into the making of cancer. But this one statement turns us myopic to more obvious reasons other than smoking and the cocktail effect of all those unrecognised factors. For the same reasons, we need to approach literacy from multiple perspectives and with the outcomes in mind rather than the input or intervening variables. The one outcome that we desire is that literacy should take us to adulthood, enable us to self-manage and enhance community, which involves:

- Reading and viewing to seeing
- Positioning oneself
- Directioning: where am I/are we going?
- Reflecting: to be human is to self-reflect
- Seeking: asking questions, digital literacy, going beyond the tools
- Bridging the conscious unconscious divide: aligning with the unconscious and the unknowable
- Sustainability: Less is more, living without stealing from the future and not leaving any footprints. Poor—rich. Community, Commons
- Shifting from the sprint to the marathon; from shooting stars to lighthouses
- Learning from doing
- Time literacy
- Science literacy
- Community intelligence (includes gender literacy)

One thing we learnt in b-school (from all those case studies) was not to look at anything with a single lens. Use as many as possible and if there is agreement between most of them, we are more likely to fare better than most.

If the lens itself is broken, we see everything as fragmented.

"How much time does it take to repair the lens?"

"24 working hours or even less."

"Why all the schooling?"

"Your parents have to go to work, come home from work and in between they have to pretend that they work. They also do not know what to do with you if you are not sent to school."

"True"

Our models of the world—The eagle's gift

As we saw in the tale of the eagle and the frog in the well in Chapter 1, the eagle swooped into the well one morning and grabbed a little frog in its talons and rose up into the sky. Then, the eagle let go of the frog right above the well. While falling back, the frog had just a glimpse of the world outside. The eagle went back to the tree and waited for the sun to set to hear the story of the day. What will be the story of the day? Tell us.

We have been collecting these stories since the very beginning. Initially, everyone connects to it in their own ways. Some identify themselves with the eagle and some with the frog and the fear of death. Not many with both— the system A and B (Kahneman), eagle and the frog, the big and the small, telescope and the microscope, Hubble and the Femtoscope, global and local, and the connections in between. How mental models are formed and revised to become mental maps?

How best to continually learn and how does the old world of the frog collapse or do the new frames come to sit on the older version of the software. A new world is born. Yet we are all in the same well—of Nature.

We will never see all of it, but we can see much more now than at any time in the past and there is a long way to go on that road.

Knowledge architecture

Meenakshi: "Explain knowledge architect"

Wanderer finds the word "awesome"

Knowledge Architecture is Knowledge + Design

Designed to?

Accelerate community learning

Create a more desirable future

Targeted at problem-specific solutions

Deliver sustained improvements

Facilitate dialogue

Most often, solutions do not lead to net improvements. The provider turns myopic to the issue out of a natural bias to one's own baby, driven by selfishness rather than appropriate selfishness (Charles Handy), creates leaders and followers, teachers and students amounting to more of dependence than independence and interdependence.

Knowledge is the sum of all that we know, will know and can know and the process is learning. To learn is to connect, reflect and catalyse—better, faster and deeper and improve together. Parents and teachers desire that children learn faster. Managers desire that they learn faster than the competition. Citizens wish that the country positions itself as a learning community and improves faster.

Do we really learn? If the outcome is improvement towards the true normal, we don't.

There is extreme urgency for rapid learning in the context of environmental concerns, social divides, growth vs. inequity, war for/liberation of talent, inclusiveness and the role of corporations in creating a more desirable future. Technical connectivity enhances the possibility of real time collective and purposive learning. Complexity of these issues demands a new pedagogy, tools and processes. More of the same will not suffice. It is not that we may not know. It is also equally important to design new ways of prioritising, showing, experiencing and comprehending what we already know at a greater scale and pace.

Knowledge architecture (KA) addresses issues of crafting new ways of seeing, a prerequisite to creating a more desirable future.

Architecture is about spaces, KA is about virtual spaces. There are many ways to achieve this.

'Visemiotics' is one.

Symbols facilitate easier navigation than written text as in the case of the graphical user interface or GUI of computers and software applications. 'A picture is worth a thousand words' is an understatement. Most often, there is no substitute for a visual symbol as in the case of road signs. Some aspects can only be communicated through visual symbols and text often hides the big picture. The younger generation depends more on visuals than on any other stimuli for learning. The visual stimuli have the highest bandwidth too. Yet, one cannot ignore anyone since each one has their own preferences. Stories, storytelling, scenarios, dream work, models, experiential learning, open space, real time management development, dialogues, a plethora of tools are available to take care of the process.

The integral FD framework is a visual tool, a product of knowledge architecture to accelerate learning and mastery of a set of high performance competencies.

Limits to Growth OR Limits to Learning?

I would like to play god for a few minutes and find and replace the word teacher with facilitator from the soft tissue memory banks of all humans and then go to sleep with the satisfaction of having done a good day's work. The collective amnesia would make sure that the word is not revived.

It is hard to stop being teachers and bring learning back to centre stage. I thank the teachers who did it for me. I also thank those who drove me to write this. But for them I wouldn't have. When I look out of the room I'm writing in, I can see the Bangalore campus of the National Dairy Research

Institute, once the Imperial Dairy Research Institute, started in 1923 by the British. Mahatma Gandhi had been there, a student for a week. That was much before my time (1971-73). What he learnt in one week, I wouldn't have learnt in two years. He would have foreseen the white revolution that would sweep across independent India.

The first learning point, the most important turning point in my life happened here. I discovered the fun of learning which had disappeared during my formal education. Disillusioned with the world of work, I returned to Bangalore as a b-school student for another two years, 1981-83. What was then the outskirts of the city is almost the heart of the city now. I was once again in Bangalore; my third time. The National Games Village, where I lived during my third stint in the city, was once a marshy swamp. The locality around, Koramangala, is more than home to the techies in Bangalore. In between, the IT revolution took off and reached its peak paving the way for the next revolution in the making. I visualise Bangalore driving that revolution—the emergence of a learning community that renews itself continually, where work, learning and leisure come together as one so that work becomes its own reward. Goodbye to incentives and stock options?

Every time I am back in Bangalore, I get a fresh lease of life and at 60, it is happening once again. There was a campaign going on in Bangalore a while back—'Teach India'. I wish they'd called it 'Learn India, Learn'. We put on our teacher's hat all too often, at home, at work, on the road and even in our dreams. We kill the joy of learning when we set out to teach; the more the teachers the less the learning. Learning can now be outcome-based on a need to know basis. The best of my teachers did the least teaching. They created the conditions for us to learn.

We had a wonderful pair, in b-school, who did the least teaching. We called them Laurel and Hardy. They allowed us to put on the teaching hats and listened to us. I was hooked to system thinking (not systems thinking) which was another learning/turning point in my learning curve. Habits seldom die. It took me three years of teaching to say goodbye to my 'teaching career' in 1984. I found myself unfit for the job, fished out my learner's hat and got wedded to LLL or life long learning. When we do that, growing old is something to look forward to. Julia Roberts, the *Pretty Woman* actress echoes it.

Growing old is becoming free. *Development as Freedom* (Amartya Sen) is true in this context also, but it is dependence for those who do not, stuck at the learning plateaus.

I remember the learning plateaus during my formal education, adolescence, at work and after work. I am not one of those Rushdie's midnight's children. I was conceived and born in a free India (1949) a baby boomer. Like most baby boomers I too grew up/down as a confused child. My early reading only added to that confusion. Those writers have now grown old and changed their positions many times over. Not many returned, like the prodigal son, to connect to their roots. Most remain still confused and they go on confusing others. The revolutions died very young leaving many casualties in the process. The orthodox Christian religious atmosphere, at home, school and all around also contributed to the making of the prodigal son. I was lucky to break out of that stifling world to rediscover the fun of learning, to get unstuck and move ahead from the plateaus of learning that came—at intervals—over the years.

The process is not always very pleasant. Bangalore is also the suicide capital of the country and the incidence is the highest among those in the age group 15-44. There is pain and suffering while we are stuck and the joy and freedom of getting unstuck from the plateaus are abundant compensation for the pain. Having gone through the process, it was a logical next step to take position as a student/facilitator of learning. One can certainly make the process easier for those interested in transcending the barriers to learning.

We started with facilitating children in schools and moved up the levels to the 'top of the pyramid' with our facilitation tools. Our prevalent notions of intelligence encourage and support the notion that a few are exceptionally gifted and fit to survive. For those who fail to be recognised as such, school can be a torture machine that kills the joy of learning, creating the first learning plateau. It is also the stage when adolescents are assumed to turn adults. When the species in general does not encourage adult behaviour and maturity, transformation to the adult is a near impossibility. The emphasis on teaching as against learning arises from the position that the majority cannot learn and therefore need to be taught. It is self-fulfilling and the adult is less likely to take birth. The first and basic distortion of the meaning drive is already seeded which gives rise to the primary learning plateau.

When we moved the facilitation process to the world of work, we found that the first plateau is instrumental in creating other barriers in the world of work. The formal education system seldom meets the expectations of the employer. The employer has to create the conditions for continual learning, more so in the context of a 'knowledge society' in emergence. Work is seldom perceived as learning or expression of one's self with the result that most get burnt out in the process. Once again, it is only a minority who manage to break through the glass ceiling. For the majority, another plateau is in the making. Meanwhile our young man/woman has become a parent and is bogged down by more responsibilities and expectations at work and home. The context is ripe for the classic symptoms of the mid-life crisis to surface. Some transcend the plateau and continue to be productive beyond their 50s. The individual and society suffer from the consequences. In large hierarchical governance systems, it is tragic to see bright, outstanding, young individuals progressively grow out of touch with reality, creating more plateaus/barriers to the collective journey of improvement and renewal. The circle is complete.

One can go on ad nauseum (the teacher is still alive). To sum up:

We have created a giant wheel. A few drive the wheel. They promise better and better rides. A few refuse to be taken for a ride. Habit is thus the enormous fly-wheel of society, its most precious conservative agent (William James-1890).

The conclusion is simple. Limits to growth = Limits to learning

The burden of normality

Our perception of normality is abnormal. This is the burden that we carry. The understanding of the true normal liberates us from this burden.

On 12 October 1492 Columbus arrived in America. The day is celebrated as Discovery Day in the Bahamas. Vasco da Gama reached Calicut, Kerala, in South India on 20 May 1498. It was a coincidence that Columbus reached America while looking for India. It took six more years of effort for the map to be completed and the mission accomplished.

Ancient Chinese seafarers probably had better maps, but history was shaped elsewhere. Galileo was struck by the bolt from the blue, but complete acceptance came centuries later.

We need a new set of maps for the next phase of the journey. Most maps waste our time and effort. If we have a unified map, it would point us to the solution space. The ship is ready, but the captain is waiting for the map.

Maps are many and they multiply exponentially. Aggregation and synthesis within domains and disciplines does happen, but less so between disciplines.

Meta maps reduce the search effort to choose the appropriate map/s for one's journey as an individual, as members of particular communities and for the collective journey of human progress.

Environment, development and sustainability are critical and complex concerns that call for concerted community action across the planet. Simple solutions and quick fixes aggravate the problems.

Every scientist faces the problem of communicating his work within the shortest span of time to the widest audience, which points to the complexity of communicating science to the masses in contexts where there is no substitute for reason and collective action.

The GUI, essentially a map and a pointer to possible virtual journeys, took computers to living rooms across the planet. The web and the cloud open up vast libraries of information and knowledge.

The visual framework discussed here was evolved in the process of addressing the environmental, developmental and sustainability challenges in the state of Kerala in India while working with livelihood and food security issues in primary production (livestock and fisheries) to evolve institutional systems to address them.

The framework was later put to use in addressing similar issues in one of the largest information technology infrastructure projects to connect local communities for development and governance and in schools, industry and academia as a tool for facilitation of accelerated organisational/community learning.

Beyond the burden of 'normality'

26 December 2004

We were rushing to Cape Comorin/Kanyakumari, the southern tip of peninsular India; two families on a holiday.

Fishermen on the high seas were casting their nets.

People in other parts of the world were asleep, dreaming good and bad dreams

The tsunami was wreaking havoc on the shores of Cape Comorin and on other shores.

We knew about the tsunami when the police blocked us on the road.

Most fishermen on the high seas knew when they returned to the shore.

Many never knew.

When we ride much bigger waves spanning centuries, we are most likely to take them for granted. It is Procrustean to catch a giant wave into the bell curve in the time span of a snapshot sans the ripples that the wave creates. So is writing a book about it, the damage is permanent. The trees are already dead.

Time is a better judge of our power trips.

Copy CATs do not catch mice.

Black or white, intelligent or idiots, they should catch mice. They do, in China, it seems.

This happened here in India, the Biggest Bazaar, with due apologies to KB.

Why do we have to clone cats when we make the best mousetraps? Let us clone the very best cats, go for a biotech solution rather than a manufacturing one. It was decided that we will have an Indian solution and the CAT came to be. The first centre was so successful that beating the CAT became the ultimate dream of the slumdog billions. Every panchayat wanted to have one such centre. A task force was constituted to decide the exact number to be set up.

There was this farmer from pre 'territorial independence' days who had four sons and five daughters. One of those five daughters had four daughters herself, and Nuthan was the youngest of them. Of the four idiots, three went to the IITs and one took a short cut to one of the CAT centres. Nuthan wanted to prove that she was a better idiot than the rest.

One cool January morning Nuthan calls:

"Hi, I cleared the CAT and am called to all the centres."

"Congratulations, you will soon be the newsmaker of 2011."

"Why?"

"You are one among 206,000, almost a Black Swan. We need to wait before concluding that we are getting mature going by the 15% drop in numbers from the previous year.

You deserve the Miss India talent crown. To the best of my knowledge you never went to school or college, but spent most of those years in indoor stadiums all over the country, having a ball. You never picked up any quant other than balancing the financial statements in your B.Com. finals. Yet you did better than the best of the astute and studious. What was your percentile?"

"99.2"

"Nuthan, you are the cutest of all the cats. All the top cats with a perfect 100 belong to the male of the species, went to IITs, went to school every single day, did their coaching circus and most of them took more than one shot to make it. You don't figure anywhere here and you have a work ex of three years playing for the oil company which you claim to have been working for and getting paid by."

"Thank you. I am scared whether I will convert the calls or not. Will you give me some tips to make it to the finals, clearing the GDPI (for the uninitiated this expands to Group Discussion and Personal Interview)."

"If you can bell the CAT without going to the circus you can as well do this without me. You should be scared that they will make you conform."

"I know you have helped some to beat the CAT."

"Ok. Let me run a small test for you."

"What is the scope for more CAT cloning centres in the country?"

"Thirteen more."

"Why?"

"We already have 13 and there are only 26 letters in the 'Inglish' alphabet. Taking the UID route will kill the unique value proposition of the brand. One should not kill the golden goose."

"Good, you are already half way there to half the centres."

"What is Indian about the Indian Institute of CATs."

"I don't know."

"Very good, that is why you are going there. You are almost there for 75% of the centres."

"Next one; suppose they ask what if you don't make it this year?"

"I will show them my GRE score which is even better than my CATS and tell them that 'you will have to face me next year with still better CATS'."

"Congratulations Nuthan, you will convert all the calls."

"Here is the last one. Suggest a few titles for the passage above."

'Normalisation and the True Normal'

'Copy cats Do not Catch Mice'

'The Bell Curve in Indian Life'

'The Fourth Idiot'

'Talent Mania and The War For Talent'

'What is Indian about the Indian Institutes of Management?'

'MCPs and the Revenge of the Underdogs'

"Great, don't go back to school. They will make you conform to the other idiots, crucify = normalise you on the Procrustean bed. Gates and Zuckerman and the other natives of the connected world graduated from the market, nothing but a different version of the same. Copy cats do not catch mice."

Nuthan: "What is Indian about the IIMs?"

"I don't know, dear."

"Thanks." (Thank God, I didn't go to school)

Similitude to living and dead CATs is intentional.

Thou shall not judge, but . . .

The Procrustean is the bedrock of modernity (mediocrity), the generator of pyramids and the hierarchical. Procrustus is a monomaniac, a Narcissus who sees that he fits his frame perfectly and uses the same to sit in judgment. I am intelligent and the other is less intelligent. I am normal and the other is fit for the madhouse. I am civilised and the other is primitive. I am a native and you are an immigrant. Mine is the only faith that guarantees salvation. He is the economist who says the American is 35 times more 'developed', since the Indian has an average income of $1,000 against $35,000 for the American. Has anybody met the average Indian or the average American? The happiness index is outside his frame of reference.

Our Mr Talent does not take to fools easily. He thinks the mainstream media is trash. To reply to the fools who read his books is not worth his time, the real resource according to his own frame. He finds his dollar worth pocketing since that is the price he fixes himself for his intellectual accomplishments. He declares himself a flaneur, a black swan, a prophet in the making.

Prophets 'normally' come from the East. Lao Tsu, Buddha, Christ, Mohammed, Sankara (from Kerala). Our Mr Talent could be a candidate for the elite corps of black swans. The rest of us are white swans. That sums up the HIStory of 2,500 years.

Prophets can be understood only against their contexts. Christ and the society which created him are so interdependent, that to strip them and to judge them in isolation is Procrustean. So are Lao Tzu, Buddha, Prophet Mohammed and Sankara. Black makes sense only against the white.

Mr Talent, the immigrant, rides the American wave better than the natives, beating the natives at their own game and nearly transforms himself to a bridge figure. Uprooted by the Procrustean and forced to flee; let us hope that he will not sacrifice himself on the bed of Procrustes.

Malcolm Gladwell starts on a very promising note highlighting how community contributes to the health of the people of Roseto Valfortore in Italy, but very soon succumbs to the compulsions of conforming to the recipe to make it to the best-seller list and goes after what constitutes the success cocktail.

All of them are male. This is part of the reason why we have the silent unseen wars between the female and the male, the unconscious against the conscious, the revenge of the underdogs, and why the 'built to last' fall apart no sooner than they are built.

Black Swans or Black Sheep?

Throughout I refer to people, not books. The books take us to the people since work defines the person. In the same spirit we look at the living rather than those long dead and still not buried. What we see depends on where we stand; our positions. One could take the Wall Street perspective or the Bangalore perspective. The black swan from the New York perspective turns out to be a black sheep from the Bangalore position.

Parts of this chapter were circulated to the tribe. The comments:

Does normal exist? Yes, when we are true to the design, we are truly normal. It has nothing to do with the fleeting 'normality of the time'. The compulsion to conform to this stupid normality is the burden of normality.

Based on the 'normal' perspective Nuthan would not get through CAT. She did not tread the beaten path. Exceptions point to the truly normal and only the truly normal can aspire to be super normal.

P.S. 19 April 2011: Nuthan calls again. She did make it to the one she wanted.

Placebos and power lies

Power Lie = Placebo + Potency!

"How can we enhance the potency of placebos?"

"Ceremonial magic, illegibility, infusion of extreme technology, semantic profligacy, misinformation overdrive, the printed word, the war for talent, intellectualise, all the Ps in marketing, pyramids, heightened threat perceptions, disciplinary silos . . . Creativity is the limit."

"Is this by design?"

"Partly by default, partly by design and mostly driven by what could euphemistically be termed as appropriate selfishness. One might even justify it with the adage—The road to hell is paved with good intentions."

"If we spoke a different language, we would perceive a somewhat different world,"—Wittgenstein.

"Language is not the only culprit. Each one of us has a different position and what we see from that position is our personal truth, which creates a world of our own in us. There is also a part of this world that fits with those of others in bits and pieces and a lot that we agree on collectively. But for the semantic confusion that follows from our variant positions, art, science, philosophy and religious texts would have dematerialised and we would have seen more in common than in isolation."

"Is it possible to take a common position so that the members of the community or the species see the same and talk the same?"

"It is possible, but it hurts. People might come to know that the most powerful medicine is just a placebo."

"The container has become the content, media the message and the massage! When everything is a lie, lie detectors are akin to mousetraps where rats are extinct. What we need is a truth detector."

Philosophy ought to be that touchstone to detect truth.

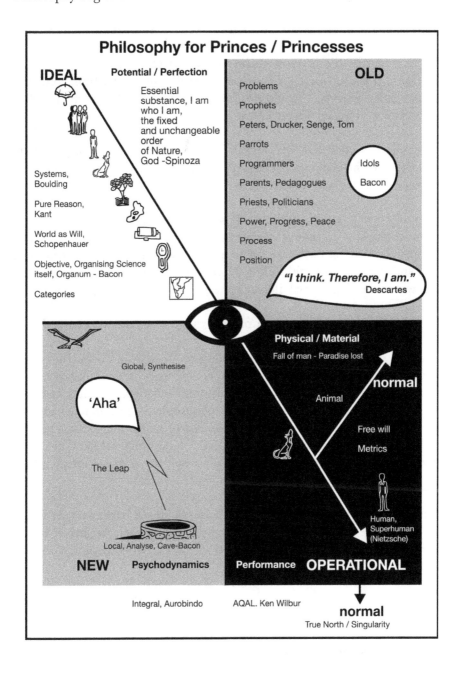

True normality

When one's inheritance is from the cloud everyone is a prince or a princess.

Will Durant tells the *Story of Philosophy* in over 600 pages and Kant takes 800 pages for the *Critique of Pure Reason*. Yet the story is far from complete. Schopenhauer laments, "I could not find a shorter way of imparting it than this book, *The World as Will and Idea*."

Philosophy has gone out of fashion. We should not expect the princes to wade through the semantic swamp of philosophy and the other disciplines and come up with a new synthesis.

The shorter way, a new synthesis, is an imperative. 'A picture is worth a thousand words' is an understatement that discounts the value of maps and mapping. Text can never be free of slipperiness and linearity. We need more maps and pictures to avoid killing more trees, more so when reading has given way to viewing. Visual literacy has become a critical competency.

The perceived normal is the abnormal. We can now see the truly normal.

History is philosophy in motion according to Benedetto Croce. Pull down the tent poles of space and time, history and philosophy collapse to the present and the two meet. The true historian (all history is lies and it is always 'his' story not 'hers' and western philosophy is no different) and the true philosopher would meet at this moment of truth. The artist, scientist, theologian and the pursuers of other paths too would meet at the same crossroads if the synthesis is effective. We would be saving a lot of wasted effort when all of us use the same philosopher's compass.

Most of our partners in dialogue have backgrounds in business, governance and developmental management. We worked together to arrive at the common ground since it is from here that accelerated community learning takes off.

Less is more.

Learning plateaus: Teachers' day out

A teacher student dialogue:

S: "Good morning, happy Teachers' Day. No classes, hurray!"

T: "Thanks, I didn't know. You seem to be very happy that you don't have classes. If teaching is about learning you wouldn't celebrate it this way. Learning itself ought to be the best fun."

S: "The teachers threw a party for us and let us off for the day."

T: "How can teachers not teach? It is unethical, against nature to strike work. A farmer cannot strike work, the cow cannot. How can a few take such freedom?"

S: "Hmm . . . . Do you think teaching in class is the only way to teach. I have learnt much more from my dreams than from class."

T: "Why should there be any teaching? Chris says they have only one word 'hweil'—in Welsh—for teaching and learning. We should have only learners and no teachers."

S: "One thing . . . quite weird, about the dreams."

T: "Shoot straight. Do not beat around the bush in your usual style."

S: "I see a dream where people only die or dreams that revolve only around my world."

T: "You never told me about these deaths other than killing your father and grandpa."

S: "Yeah. Last night I saw two babies killed. I did not kill them, but they died, one of them as soon as it was born and the other after a few months."

T: "What was the dream?"

S: "I forgot if I was the mother or not. All I remember is that children died. I was sad though I did not cry. I don't remember any more."

T: "You are stuck at 13. That is the reason for the killings, grow up. You are not yet an ADULT to have babies."

S: "I saw that someone said these children would have survived if you were 26."

T: "It shows."

S: "Yeah, very right, amazing."

T: "Great learning. Now take a break, here is a story that came in my mail right now, synchronicity?"

A turkey was chatting with a bull. "I would love to be able to get to the top of that tree," sighed the turkey, "but I haven't got the energy."

"Well, why don't you nibble on some of my droppings?" replied the bull. "They're packed with nutrients."

The turkey pecked at a lump of dung and found it actually gave him enough strength to reach the lowest branch of the tree.

The next day, after eating some more dung, he reached the second branch.

Finally, after a fourth night, the turkey was proudly perched at the top of the tree. He was promptly spotted by a farmer, who shot him out of the tree.

Moral of the story: Bull poop might get you to the top, but it won't keep you there.

T: "So how do you move from 13 to 22?"

S: "I don't know."

T: "You are stuck at a learning plateau, like most of us. We are all stuck at different plateaus when we are on the well-travelled road, the linear in the visual. Take the non-linear road if you do not want to get into highway pile-ups. According to the model, the other plateaus are around 35-40 and 55-60 years, the mid-career and senior levels. There may be exceptions who take their own road very early."

S: "As I study, I see my competitors. Earlier I saw myself studying. It is different now. I see killing or trying to murder them. That is evil, isn't it?"

T: "What goes here?"

S: "Why the smile?"

T: "It is easy to see physical aggression. There is a more dangerous version that goes unnoticed. You are in the process of killing the Hitler in you."

Time for another break, so here's another story:

An eagle was sitting on a tree doing nothing.

A small rabbit saw the eagle and asked him, "Can I also sit like you and do nothing?"

The eagle answered: "Sure, why not."

So, the rabbit sat on the ground below the eagle and rested. All of a sudden, a fox appeared, jumped on the rabbit and ate it.

T: "You are killing because you are stuck. You are killing yourself, refusing to be an adult. What should be the trajectory under ideal conditions from 13 to 21, teen to the adult? I am not talking about chronological aging."

S: "Yeah, mm . . . physical changes, changes in thoughts and perception."

T: "What about the most basic drive, meaning or purpose in life? Has it been resolved? Why are you here? This is the first plateau."

S: "Yeah, I think we discussed it when we discussed Maslow and I am fairly clear about it. I know why I am here."

T: "Physical changes will happen even without our consent. Nature is good at that but we are more than our physical selves. The mental and spiritual growth challenges need be resolved if you are not to be confused and remain stuck at perpetual adolescence."

S: "You tell me. I am clueless I guess."

T: "Most of us are confused about the role of sex and sexuality to resolve the emotional challenges at this stage of one's growth. The distortion stays till the end. Even before Christ we had the Kama Sutra. After 2,200 years we are not ready to discuss it, sex and sexuality, in schools or families or even between 'adults'."

S: "Hmm . . . That is right; I wish I were wiser."

T: "Sex is the most difficult drive to be managed. First and foremost it is a spiritual thing. If you accept the spirituality of it, it cannot do any damage and it will eliminate the commoditisation of sex. It is a natural drive. It is not for just reproduction. Reproduction is not such a big issue. Anyway we have more numbers than we want for survival of the species. Had it been just for reproduction, nature would have designed it the animal way. Earlier we had mentioned trisexual men and women."

S: "Yeah, I remember."

T: "One cannot be sexual with somebody else if one is asexual with oneself. This is like Christ said; love your SELF to love your neighbour. So the first step is to accept and appreciate the drive in itself so that one can express the same to the other. The other could be from the same sex or the opposite. Now you know what tri-sexual is, self, the other, male, female."

T: "What about marriage? The young ones of the species take the longest time to grow up. In addition, this meets the learning requirement for humans. One can learn only in relationship with another person who will not run away from you."

S: "I did not get it exactly, I am confused."

T: "If you are not in such a relationship you will never know your blind spots, like I know how immature or mature I am only when I look at my relationships at home, because we cannot take such liberties in our outside relationships. So marriage and family is for learning and adulthood and once this is achieved, the institution is redundant. For a long time to come this is quite unlikely. Marriage is for mortals."

T: "This is the seeding for future dreaming and for transcending the adolescence plateau so that the bonsai becomes the tree."

S: "But, you know, I think . . . I felt very comfortable to remain a baby."

T: "Now the dreams should change. The bonsai is happy, people would admire it but the design is not for that. This is why we don't have adults in this world, in spite of all the teachers, including Christ and Buddha."

T: "So wallow, more bull poop, remain a baby?"

S: "Gosh. No . . . well, I don't know many who are adults the way you ask them to be, I guess."

T: "Probably there are no adults when we look from the position of the species. We are very immature as a species and more threatened than the animals. When the species is not mature how can any one of us be an adult?"

S: "Once I thought, It is disgusting and a pain to remember my dreams."

T: "I know and you resisted very strongly. Cows align north-south when they graze and even when they sleep."

S: "Hmm. Why do they do so?"

T: "They have a built in GPS. They know the direction; they are more comfortable when they are in alignment, in tune. Animals are always in tune. You are a singer and a guitarist. You should know."

S: "Why is it that we don't know how to tune ourselves, SELVES?"

T: "This is the problem with free will. Animals have no choice. We have options and we need to exercise choice. We have to choose the direction. They are naturally tuned, as far as we guess, and we don't know how to choose. We too have a compass, but just having it does not mean that we use it."

S: "Hmm . . . then we are worse than animals, it seems they are more intelligent or may be luckier?"

T: "What makes us different from the animal?"

S: "Brains, as everyone says or may be a sense of humour?"

T: "This is tragic. You know everything, but not this simple thing. People are very smart, they are quiz masters, know everything under the sun or can Google it and get the information. But we are bad about such simple stuff. None has answered us within 10 seconds. So smarty, give me the answer or admit defeat."

S: "I admit defeat! Surrender. Well, one more guess. We choose to go the way others have not gone, while animals keep going on."

T: "I want the unique difference between animals and the human. We don't choose is what I am saying. To choose we should know and we don't know; non ADULTs, how can you choose then? You had so many teachers, hats off to all of them on Teachers' Day. They did not teach you this!"

S: "May be they did not choose to teach this."

T: "We are the only species that can improve; others cannot. Animals cannot improve, we can but we don't."

S: "Yeah, right."

T: "Ok. Happy dreaming. Now you will see the dreams evolve and the alignment with the internal and external will follow. Bye. Take care."

S: "Thank you. Bye."

War for talent vs. Liberation of talent

India is one of the top remittance-receiving countries in the world, with annual remittances of Rs 128,500 crores, which is more than the defence expenditure of the country. Kerala and Tamil Nadu account for half of the total migrants. The bulk of remittances are from West Asia, contributed by semiskilled and unskilled labour. The demographic profile of migrants is in transition and the next generation of new entrants to the job market need skills and competencies of a different order Enhancing employability through investments in skill training is assigned a very high priority in turning the demographic liability into a demographic dividend.

Over 600,000 B.Tech/MCAs and 2,000,000 other graduates pass out every year from colleges in the country. The number of engineering graduates is more than double that of graduates who pass out of all US universities. The lure of employment rather than aptitude influences the decision to go to college. Even a professional degree is not always a passport to a certain job.

Employability is the capability to gain initial employment, maintain employment and obtain new employment if required. The war for talent (WFT) model pre-supposes that there is only a limited pool of outstanding talent. A few can make a larger difference and that they are more fit to survive. They flock to IITs and IIMs as part of their strategy to outsmart the competition. The media creates headlines when the Indian Institute of Science, Bangalore secures a global ranking of 35 in employability. Nobody is keen to know its ranking in science-ability.

The liberation of talent model is based on a different set of assumptions. It recognises that the problems of intelligence and knowledge have changed. There is not a limited pool of innate talent. The major problem in a developing context is creating the conditions for the liberation of talent of the masses in agriculture and the unorganised sectors of the economy, leveraging the potential of new technologies, which calls for new ways of approaching the management of talent.

A case is often made to establish that there exists a wide gap between what industry wants and what education institutions offer, though both sides are equally illiterate of the different positions and perspectives that go into the noise.

The terminology of 'hard' and 'soft' skills best illustrates this ambiguity about skills, competencies and performance. It is said that for people working in technology the 'hard' skills include technical competencies—skills that are obtained through formal education and hands-on learning, which are measureable and learnable and need to be constantly renewed. 'Soft' skills on the other hand are generally interpersonal competencies that are more difficult to define and measure. While one may, for example, learn to make a bomb, even get some practical training in this respect and also get certified to the effect, no consideration is made as to the mental framework of the student. But it is the mental framework—the 'soft' skills—and attitudes together that decide whether the bomb adds value or adds costs (9/11).

The truth is hard skills are soft and soft skills are hard and once the 'soft' skills are in place, learning and acquisition of skills to suit the requirements of performance is the responsibility of the employee in an environment where adulthood and responsibility are in demand.

There exists a cultural aspect, embedded in each one of us, which often stands in the way of creating and sustaining a high performance system. Consider, for instance, something as simple as the ability to ask questions;

a competence that is essential if one is to add value in a professional, high performance organisation. Over a decade of working with b-school students, we have found them extremely reluctant to ask intelligent questions. Engineering graduates and graduates from the humanities stream who do not receive much formal training in these areas are still further down the ladder.

Competency is the state or quality of being adequately or well qualified to perform a task. While a person may have the competency to perform a task, one need not have the desire to perform.

Given the above context, it is imperative to develop an accelerated learning and competency development (ALCD) framework and methodology to address these issues on a war footing to ensure that the demographic dividend does not turn into a demographic liability. Over the years the ALCD approach has been tested and it appears that it is certainly feasible to evolve a fast track model.

The misinformation overload and another snake oil cure

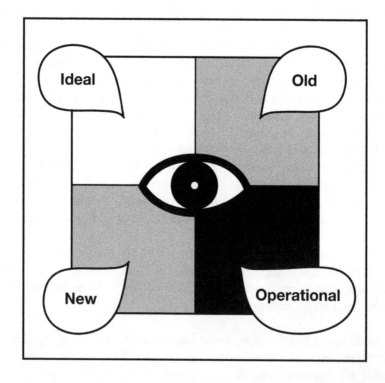

A conversation:

"It is the same wine, in a larger bottle."

"Packaging is everything in a cosmetic culture."

"You seem to be at your humorous best. It is not humour, call it pathetic humour."

"The best packaging, container, will not take care of poor content in the long run. Snake oil salesmen will make only quick bucks."

"That seems to be what business is all about! How do you separate the chaff from the grain?"

"We will first arrive at the essential content, the ideal, that which renders real value not the kind of value that marketers create out of 'appropriate selfishness'. When we club all our appropriate selfishness we get what we see."

"What do you mean?"

"The enemy within is more dangerous because all our defences are pointed towards the one outside. And though we might have all the equipment we will not be equipped to pull the trigger when it is called for because of this internal squeamishness. The emperor is naked though fully covered up by the most elaborate and intricate ornamentation."

"Is there an enemy outside?"

"It depends on the position. From a variant position, yes and from the invariant, no. There is no enemy out there. All deaths are suicides and all conversation a soliloquy."

"The ideal is an internal dress code, the bare minimum to cover up our nakedness. Once, we were discussing this issue and one of our participants had a dream of a beautiful tomb. She could also see the rotting body of the emperor inside."

"She must have been a good Christian."

"She had overheard her parents reading the Bible."

"The ideal is pure potential, perfection, reason, will, design, internal, conceptual, God for ordinary mortals, the grand design for Hawking; in essence the same content in different packaging. Re-packaging is what creates the best sellers. The semantic swamp that results appears to be information at first glance."

"Let us get back to the roots. Sanskrit means processed, civilised, cultured as against Prakrit, the primitive, unprocessed. The essential content is the output of this processing that goes on; something that is perennial, universally relevant, beyond time and space, 'akshaya', immortal, culture or the ideal. We need to be clear on this to master separating the chaff from the grain."

"This is the most essential competency to survive today."

"Why flout all the rules of grammar and convention?"

"Sanskrit was the language of processing at one time. We need a new language of processing and our language experts suggested Inglish. Inglish does not have the world view that goes with English nor most of its rules of grammar. It is a common, purpose-oriented language, which retains the essence. Most memories and conventions keep us tied down to the past."

"So how does this competency take care of the information overload?"

"Information overload is a misnomer since the very character of information is that it kills variety and reduces the overload. It increases the order, fights decay and death. It is life giving. We might call this data overload which is a boon to the storage industry and to those who put all their faith in more power to the machines and less to the humans in general, but not necessarily to an elite few."

"We need some kind of meta information about information itself."

"Ravana, the emperor, has ten heads; quite a burden for most practical purposes. The ideal is mapped under ten heads in the call out in the top left quadrant of the First Discipline Framework. We have ten balls within that one ball."

"You are making it more complicated? All those ten heads didn't really help him."

"All complexity is not a curse. Requisite complexity and variety are unavoidable. Miss out on any one of the recipe's ingredients and the dish goes to the garbage dump."

"Why ten?"

"Ten is the minimum requisite variety to understand the basic design, the master templates of nature."

"What do these ten heads stand for?"

"Let us take the information head. The information head is information about information. In the absence of this information one will not be able to transform data to information and reduce the complexity. Misinformation overload is the result."

"Another example:

$2x2 = 4, 4x4 = 16, 16x16 = 256, 256x256 = ?$

The multiplication table ceases to serve the purpose at a certain stage of increasing complexity. All tools reach this limit and at some stage the wheel needs to be reinvented. Reinventing is a new synthesis. It is relevant in other contexts too. When one has a major accident, on the road or off, it is time for a new synthesis. There are always better solutions and the best is always yet to come. Even health and healing is more about information than about medicines."

"Now a little more meditation on the ten will give you all the clues. You are on your own."

"Why always leave a large part of it unexplained?"

We need to break from treating others as children, like all governments do, and relate as adults so that the adult emerges. We point to the issue and one has to figure it out for oneself if it has to be of any use."

Knowledge visualisation

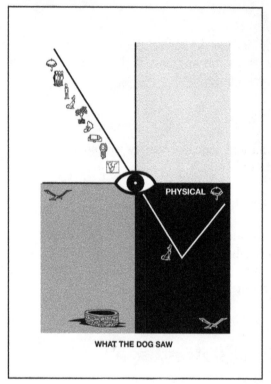

Visualising knowledge:

From the lowly perspective of a dog's eyes, everyone looks short—Chinese proverb

From knowing to SEEing

All dogs do not see the same.

Stray dogs see better than domesticated dogs.

The latter become less intelligent in the process; levelling?

They may not be very 'lowly' as the Chinese say.

We haven't fared any better than them.

On community intelligence: Even the dog sees that we have gone astray!

Maslow revisited

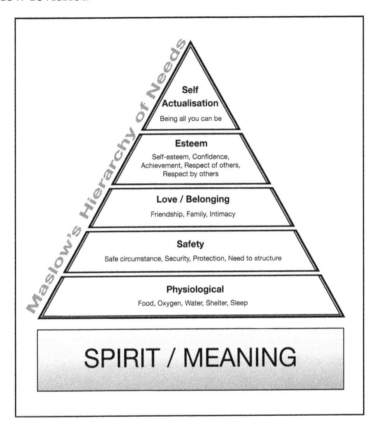

"If you have built your castles in the air your work need not be in vain, for that is where they should be. Now build foundations underneath them."—Ralph Waldo Emerson

Root wilt meets bunchy top: J has retired after working for 34 years. M is between jobs and waiting for the next call from the head hunter. He was the country head of an MNC, one of the Fortune 100, till recently.

M: "We have a 26/11, the Indian version of 9/11, and you are still digging?"

J: "Recessions, terrorism and religious fundamentalism have many things in common. It is very much part of the syndrome that we discuss. We were digging from 1981 to 1990 when the synthesis happened and the FDF fell in place. Without looking back, digging deeper into oneself and also into our collective past, we cannot go ahead. We can see ahead as much as we can see into our past. Since 1990, more than digging, we have been facilitating the process of digging and integration, one to one, in groups and for organisations."

M: "Root wilt and bunchy top?"

J: "When the soil is dying, the flora and fauna come to suffer from these attacks. The malady advances like an invading army; acres and acres of crops surrender to the advance and vanish year by year. Scientists continue to work for solutions but none have been effective. The science that we use most often is not science because the bits and bytes do not come together to address the complexity of the issue in sufficient measure. It is not only plants that suffer from bunchy tops and root wilts. We find hardly any family that has not been touched by suicide, psychiatric illness, heart attack or cancer—most often more than one of these. A suicide is very much like root wilt because the individual fails to find his roots and grow up. Psychiatric illness is another kind of root wilt because the person's efforts at making meaning out of existence leads to a crisis. The terrorist is just another version of it. Other illnesses too have a link with the primary distortion in meaning, which is at the heart of the issue. Bunchy top is the syndrome that goes with power and hierarchy—the emperor is naked."

M: "The monarchy is not dead?"

J: "Hardly. There is a change in style and fashion, superficial and cosmetic. The monarchy of Indian origin ended with emperor Ashoka. The West took it over, beginning with Alexander. He was too young to pass through the identity crisis that Ashoka had. The West has been celebrating its success since then and success corrupts more than power. When the monarchies started weakening, they got into strategic alliances with the clergy, giving rise to the wave of conversion/colonisation. The great learning from this wave was that territorial control is no more critical to staying ahead, that competitive advantage is embedded in the intangibles—concepts, design, technology, standards, market and, to be more specific, capital markets. The brain mattered more than brawn. Nations shrunk to give way to MNCs, the corporate multi 'national' 'nations' often much bigger than nations. The emperors put on different clothes. Attila the Hun, Genghis Khan, Charlemagne, the Vikings were all reinvented to be icons of fashion of the day. There is now a great rush to save the pyramids and not enough time to go digging. When we are in a great rush we fail to see what happens at home. The seniors could help because they are in no great rush. They can go digging and might come up with some treasures. Or you could outsource it to India. They are better at digging because of the greater diversity in terms of the plurality of religions, languages, colour and myriad other differentiators. It is like the Galapagos to Darwin. We might come up with a new theory of human evolution. This is the unique competitive advantage of the country that China and the US should be worried about from an obsolete leadership perspective."

J: "The pyramids continue to attract us. They have stood the test of time and are not out of our collective psyche. We now have other forms of multinational pyramids with the bottom and the top out of alignment. Recessions are the result of the tectonic shifts between the top and the bottom.

The self is to the organisation as the cell is to the body. Our maps of the cell are not yet complete. We are yet to decipher the 'junk DNA'. If we don't understand something we junk it. We don't have a map of the self, but we have so many 'working' models of mammoth organisations.

We need to really dig deeper to come out of the crisis. History seldom helps because most of it is about glorified aggression. Moreover, it cannot give us solutions since the same logic that created the problem cannot be of relevance to craft solutions to the issue."

M: "The central issue is a perennial one. You might get a glimpse of it between the logic gates."

Tower of Babel vs. leaning tower of Pisa

Ashoka vs. Alexander

The Flood and the Ark

Pyramids vs. Networks/Communities of continual self renewal

Change vs. Sustained transformational improvements

Affluenza vs. Influenza

David vs. Goliath

Free market vs. Bailouts

Creating wealth vs. Philanthropy—"Behind every great fortune is a crime,"—Honoré de Balzac (1799-1850)

M: "When we are on top of the pyramid we cannot see the bottom. Even at a much lower level, there are very few families with a sustained trajectory of improvements. One generation makes it and the next generation squanders it is a norm. We are discussing a design problem as to how this trap can be circumvented since the issue is not change, but sustained continuous improvements—building the new tower of Babel. This time we need to bring in the spirit/nature to the centre of it which is not likely to happen, going by the history of collapses. The frog will be blissfully unaware that it is turning into frog soup."

J: "A recession is natures way of bringing you back in touch with the bottom?"

M: "It is much more than that. We are taken hostage by the pirates occupying the top of the pyramids, much like the Saudi oil tanker Sirius Star with its $100 million cargo. The pyramid could be an academic discipline, a cult, a religious sect, in short wherever the ADULT and the dialogue is blocked, perhaps unintentionally."

J: "How do you differentiate, the adult from the dictator?"

M: "Watch the language. If it is one that the man on the road fails to connect to, we have reasons to worry. Leadership is not about having followers. Christ gave us a model of servant leadership, washing the feet of his disciples. Ashoka turned into a servant of the masses. Gandhi did the same. The church could not hold on to the model for long; it has become the oldest surviving pyramid. Respect for diversity: When we don't respect the diversity of the flora and fauna, nature dies. When we don't respect the diversity of the human, the species is at risk. When we put all our money in GM we are risking our financial future. It applies to faith too. The NICs, (newly industrialised countries) showed that they could follow the path taken by the US. China has already proven that they are much better at it at a much larger scale. India will not be able to do it because of its greater complexity, diversity and the improbability of the emergence of a similar leadership."

J: "I am reminded of a metaphor on leadership. Mumbai has one of the largest abattoirs in the world. When sheep are unloaded from trucks, they are lead by leader goats whose job it is to go to the trucks and lead the sheep, show them the way, through the maze of barricades. It is a long wait as the lines are very long. When the leader goats reach the butcher, they move ahead and the followers get slaughtered under the butcher's knife. At times absence of leadership is a blessing in disguise."

M: "But there has also been an unprecedented improvement in the last 100 years in real terms. We are more connected and we can see in real time much more than any time in the past. There has been a lot of shift from the static to the dynamic, more of openness and transparency, opportunities for the individual to express her SELF."

J: "The major aphorisms of the connected world are:

- The number of transistors that can be built on the same-sized piece of silicon will double every eighteen months. (The power of the chip doubles every eighteen months—Gordon Moore.)

- Value of a network rises exponentially relative to the square of the number using it—Robert Metcalfe.

- Power of creativity rises exponentially with the diversity and divergence of those connected into a network—John Kao (Chinese American Business Thinker).

The first two are already part of our experience, but the last one is the most powerful. Here lies the competitive advantage of India. Globally, here is the opportunity to leverage ourselves out of the recession and move into an altogether different phase of sustained continuous improvements as against discrete, random and isolated improvements."

M: "So the imperative is to connect at a much larger scale and transform the pyramids to continuous learning engines?"

J: "A learning engine is capable of continuously improving on its previous best performance so that there are no booms and busts as in the past. Continuous improvement implies continual learning."

M: "Why have you come up with an addendum to Abraham Maslow?"

J: "This is something that participants in FD workshops came up with. They said the model is more complete if the hierarchy of needs is placed on the foundation of the spirit. For a man who finds suicide to be meaningful, the hierarchy does not matter! It sounded very right. Probably we may have to revisit the great man."

M: "What else have they come up with in your digging workshop?"

J: "I have a mail to our dream archives from one of our participants. He had it the night after the process workshop which was about digging deeper into our selves—part of it was to connect with the male and the female in us:

'Recovery of Sita: The dream

Huge crater, mouth of the volcano, Sita takes him very close to the bottom of the crater walking down over the soft greyish golden sand to the spewing spurting jets of yellowish molten lava accumulating as fluffy sand They stand together watching the lava turning into soft sand. Though they are very close to the mouth, it is not hot at all.

They walk away from the mouth of the crater through the twilight zone holding each other close, at peace and in harmony with each other. He moves to kiss her on the lips. She too wants to, but gently restrains him leading him across the shadows to light. She stops facing him and plants the gentlest kiss on his lips. He returns the kiss. He feels truly at home and experiences a peace that he has never known before.

Sita ends her life requesting mother earth to swallow her: Myth/ History.

Rama exiles Sita to the forest, doubting her fidelity, based on logic similar to that of Julius Caesar: 'Caesar's wife must be above suspicion.' Sita was pregnant with Rama's twins. They grow up in a hermitage in the forest. Rama meanwhile performs the horse sacrifice to enlarge his empire (expanding market share?) sending out a horse accompanied by a huge army. The twins tie up the horse and defeat the army. Rama realises that the two are no ordinary children, goes to the hermitage and meets his sons for the first time. When the sons are grown up, Sita ends her life by asking mother earth to open and swallow her. She has had enough of it'."

M: "Why are you digging into dreams, fantasy and fiction once again?"

J: "They are more real and we are driven by them more than facts. Because the feminine is more difficult to connect to. We buried her long long ago in our distant past. Since the feminine is buried, the male too is a shadow of the real. The result is that the self functions like an engine with half the cylinders not firing. Moreover, the Hummer is running in reverse gear with the accelerator stuck to the floor. Somebody has played a prank with the driver's seat, fixing it in the opposite direction. The driver believes that he is doing well, blissfully unaware of heading in the wrong direction. The bystanders applaud and go on watching the feat."

J: "Recessions have been the outcome of typical male macho linearity. More of the same will take us faster to our doom, such as the bailouts. This is the time for the non-linear, waves, cycles and the spiral. The male would say 'let us cut down on the head count, on travel, training or let me get out taking my bonus'. The female would say 'let us cut down on our perks and salaries, let us not kill the community, let us transform the pyramid into a learning engine which improves itself continually, bring in radical improvements in productivity and meanwhile I will take the largest cut.'

The US is the typical male. To me, the Japanese are a better blend of the male and the female."

M: "Why look for another source of energy?"

J: "We are running out of the dirty fuels. The mixture—dirty fuels+dirty spirituality+mean business+poor governance—forms the worst explosive cocktail, threatening the survival of the species and the planet. The recession was/is a golden opportunity to take stock and reposition ourselves, to focus on the real economy of real improvements, real growth and true community. We understood the atoms and molecules and connected with one source of energy. This was no doubt a huge step in mastering the machine logic. We deciphered the DNA which was an improvement in terms of understanding the bio-logic. We understand distant space better than the deep space within us, which is turning into desert. If the deserts on land are to bloom, we need the desert in us to bloom too, bringing back nature to our centre; that from which we had moved away. The rock logic needs to be balanced with the water logic. This will be the mother of all revolutions to happen, connecting to the perennial source of clean energy. Please do not confuse this with NAN, new-age nonsense, or another version of feminism. This is about evolving a new language of performance and the dia-logic, going beyond the clichés and jargon."

M: "Another one of your obsessions seems to be about the centre."

J: "When you put some weight in one of the pans of the common weighing balance, it tilts, and when counterbalanced moves in the opposite direction. But there is no shift at the centre of the beam. When the football is being kicked around, the centre is not disturbed though a pinprick can disturb the equilibrium. The earth, other planets and the sun too have centres. There is a relationship between the centre of the earth, other planets and the centre of the sun. There may be tectonic shifts happening on the planet, but if the relationship between the two centres is broken, try to imagine the situation. The solar system has a centre, which in turn is connected to the centre of the galaxy and so on. We understand this relationship and make use of it to propel our spacecrafts to the outer reaches of space. We are talking about small and big systems of a particular class. The human is much more than such clockwork systems because we are much more than our physical self. The physical self, like all other objects, has a centre. What about the mind and the spirit? Do they too have a centre and if so how are they connected together in the self? We need to connect to this centre to keep us in balance. This is what real recession-proofing is all about."

M: "Why bring the spirit into it? We are getting into unfamiliar territory."

J: "It is very simple. How many sides, has the coin?"

M: "Two . . . three . . . many . . ."

J: "How many sides for time?"

M: "Three—past, present, future; may be more."

J: "What about the day?"

M: "Day, night, dusk and dawn. So what?"

J: "Body and mind alone are not sufficient to describe the self. It is just like the coin with two sides which cannot exist in physical reality. All the talk about the two sides of the coin will fail to materialise it. How can you describe Gandhi without a mention of what he lived and died for? So where you focus your energy is what the spirit is all about; what you find meaning in is an integral dimension of the self. The self is born when this is recognised by the self and it matures when it connects to the community self, which brings people together around such people. In the 2008 US presidential election, Barack Obama did it better than John McCain. He focused on the unfocused blue ocean space whereas McCain went for the conventional. Obama could connect to more and I wish McCain could have been the number two and brought all of 'US' together to tackle our common issues. May be the US should have two vice presidents so that the loser in the presidential election can be one of them."

M: "Are you suggesting that the self is seldom born?"

J: "Well, let us see this as a process. We may not be far from the truth to make such a conclusion going by the degree of community among us and the hyper inflation in our problems. We deny needs to the majority and glorify the wants of a minority. The pyramids tumble down in the tectonic shifts because the foundation and the top are not aligned, a part of the truth about recessions and meltdowns, booms and busts."

M: "An extension of this logic would mean that one might find killing someone to be spiritual."

J: "Well, many have found it to be so and many continue to believe in such spirituality. Established religions have not gone much farther from this position. It is dangerous to leave spirituality to religions, which have become another version of mean business. Spirituality is primarily about transcending work to play, which will unleash quantum improvements to human productivity and quality which is a kind of clean energy and energy saved is energy produced without carbon."

M: "Are you pulling Thomas Friedman's legs?"

J: "Flat, hot and crowded is a typical linear statement though most of the book is focused on the SW quadrant of the FD framework."

J: "He would do well to dig deeper into his self, taking his own prescription for the malady. He touches on the need for non-linearity. Linearity is short-run and very local. Non-linearity is process thinking, thinking in waves, cycles and the spiral. The waves will have ups and down. We cannot go completely against the cycles of nature. We need to work with them.

He claims to be an American and sees the issue as an American issue, not human or global though he can legitimately claim only to be a US citizen. We are first humans, then Americans, Chinese or Indians. Friedman seems to be first an 'American' and then a human. In Friedman's reckoning China is worth a chapter, India is worth a few names and the rest of the world does not count at all. The book seems to have been timed to coincide with the 2008 US elections."

M: "I think we will be least affected by the meltdown. We know how to live like royalty with $2 a day, under the shade of what they call the poverty line."

J: "Balu wrote from Silicon Valley that I should be discussing Paul Krugman and not Friedman. The scale and size of any of the IT 'biggies' from India would not even touch the size of the R&D budget of Microsoft and by US scale even Microsoft is not all that big. Here nobody understands scale and size. So India doesn't really figure when we discuss the global.

It also means that the masses fail to catch up with the process of reckoning. The bottom of the pyramid is out of the reckoning against the metrics of markets and money. We will soon be bottling sunshine and branding it 'Sun spirit'. Drinking water from an unpolluted river has no economic value, but when you bottle it and sell it, it adds to the GDP; if the sale is in $, the better. If I am in the bottled water business, polluting the river appeals to my shadow self. If one is a hunter or gatherer he does not count. Taking care of forests and water bodies and living lightly on such resources has no economic value since it is beyond the current systems of metrics. The more aggressive we are in our consumption, the more developed we are."

M: "When we dig deeper, we may not like all that comes up."

J: "The participants in one of the workshops came up with some footprints left by succeeding waves of globalisation. Here's an excerpt:

Jewish Synagogue—700 BCE

The Ashoka Pillar 304-232 BCE

The first teak plantation in the world 1842-44

The tropical forests and the tribal ecosystem people retreated over the last century in the march of the 'developmental process'—the onward march of teak, tea, sugar cane rubber and other plantations. The original green was replaced by the plantation green which also brought along fertilisers, pesticides and weedicides to the source of the major rivers, killing off flora and fauna. The natural processes—cycles of renewal—were broken and the soil is dying. The farmers showed us how the death of the soil marches ahead year by year as the markets expand and the crops come to suffer from 'root wilts' and 'bunchy tops'. People too come to suffer from root wilts and bunchy tops, fall ill, as they fail to connect to the roots through their head and heart."

M: "What is happening now is quite different. The opportunity is directly in proportion to the size and scale of the crisis."

J: "May be, may be not. This will depend on how we respond to the crisis as individuals and as a community. Digging deeper helps, if it leads to a new synthesis."

J: "I mailed an early version of this part of the conversation to some friends. Here are a few responses:

San says that recession-proofing at a material level is feasible if one is competent to add value continually (implies continual learning) and at a spiritual level if one knows oneself. As I see it, knowing oneself and continual learning is one and the same. He adds that facilitators and trainers are but scavengers.

Dev wrote that most of this dialogue is Greek and Latin, pointing to the issue of language and communication in our search for the common ground. He also asks a hard hitting question: When the species is yet to reach its adulthood, where are the adults to have a dialogue?"

M: "Recessions must be good for many—economists, psychologists, priests, prophets of what is wrong with the world and the illness specialists in general. At times this could lead to a spiritual problem for the practitioner. When you pay attention to entropy you come to suffer from it unless you experience negative entropy of a higher order. If illness is perceived as an opportunity, the practice is but glorified scavenging. Waste recycling of any kind, physical, mental, spiritual, could also be equally good investment opportunities. I should review my portfolio and take a position in some of these while I transition to a more stable system.

I do not want to cash in on such opportunities, but I am in it just to take care of my responsibilities. If those are taken care of, I would just quit the game and just BE what I am. Why should I become anything? I don't want to be empowered. The very word suggests that we are powerless."

J: "The tragedy is we don't see the economic value of BEING one self. The flower out there is being itself. It is not putting on a show that it is improving the world, nor does the Jersey cow which gives many times more milk than what the calf needs. All we say is that being oneself is the best economic proposition too. Let the design express itself and do not stand against it. This is the only way to bring in net improvements. It is when we go against the design that we end up with problems. If the clock gets stuck we would check the design to make it work. It is when we come across problems that we need to understand the design better. So this is the best of times to take stock of what we have done with our SELVES."

M: "But how do you know what you know about yourself is all there is to know or what we know is knowledge. I could be wallowing in the mud and claiming that all is well with my world."

J: "We need a compass for map making, as in the case of a terrestrial journey, to fix the home position and the variant positions of the journey. When we reflect on the home position with the variant positions we should be able to make sure that we are on course, that there are net improvements. Without reference to that centre and anchoring to the centre we will continue to be afflicted by the bipolar syndrome. When the species itself is afflicted, there is only a degree of difference between the normal and the abnormal in their polarities."

M: "So what next, after principles, people and positions?"

J: "We are not through with People, Position, Positioning and Positions. We need to clarify our common position, the invariant one, the lighthouse position or the home position, where we really belong. The centre in each one of us where all of us are connected, which could lead to the emergence of community. This is something like a foreign body inside the pearl oyster around which the pearl material accumulates."

M: "You are suggesting that community does not exist now and that we are centre less."

J: "When the sheet of rubber is pulled evenly in all directions the centre remains at the centre as far as the sheet remains one. When the sheet becomes a football, the centre shifts to the centre of the football. There is no rubber at the centre. It remains as such even when kicked around the field. All it takes is a pinprick to throw the centre out of whack.

We are yet to get rid of the flat earth maps. The popular metaphor is flatter, hotter, crowded and so on."

M: "If there is something like a home position that all of us can agree to, what would that be?"

J: "The central issue is what is it to be human; the unique differentiator from other categories of life? Over the years many have come to agree that the differentiator is our Potential to improve and improve continually. Would you agree?"

M: "There goes one more of your Ps—Potential. You have some kind of fixation with Ps. My psychologist friend of the Freudian school has a different name for it.

I agree tentatively so that the dialogue continues as I don't see continual improvement anywhere around. I see only booms and busts and sporadic improvements. On the whole I am tempted to conclude that net improvements have been negative."

J: "It is not wrong to have some fixations, invariance, where people too often preach that change is the only constant. Values and principles are immortal. Another one could be—to be human is to improve and improve continually to realise more and more of the Potential, both personal and collective. Not to improve is sub-animal. This is where we are a class apart from the animal. The root cause of our Problems (another P) is the unrealised potential, which drives us to all the substitutes, the bulk of our products and services. One reason why the markets are shrinking is that people eventually come to know that these were substitutes and might choose not to consume more of them as they mature. Recessions can be partly explained by this logic."

J: "From a different perspective, there has been no recession of our problems, in spite of all the solution providers, total and partial, the common position taken by Priests, Politicians, Pedagogues and Parents. The truth is that we have hyper inflation in the scale and magnitude of our problems in spite of all the Progress, which brings us to the issue of what is true progress—improvement or Performance. When you sum up, net improvements might be negative over centuries. The ecological footprint is a pointer to this. Business takes the position that they have either a product or service or a mix of both as the solution to a problem. The issue is what your business is. If one is in the business of shadows and substitutes, one will not be free from booms and busts whereas if one is in the business of continually creating net improvements continual growth follows. The same holds good at the level of individuals too.

The sub-animal is much worse than the animal. Animals have better community and they don't kill within the community without rhyme or reason. They are true to their potential whereas though we have the potential we do not realise it. If we are unhappy about our collective behaviour, the central reason is we seldom connect to our true potential nor do we have any clues as to our true potential; not that any of us do not want to improve. In the process, we turn sub-animal in our behaviour. Animals sense whether we are human or sub-animal. In extreme cases, they express it too. Somebody I know was chased by dogs on the beach. His only option was to get into the water. The dogs waited on the beach, howling. He was rescued by the guards on the beach, but committed suicide shortly thereafter."

M: "So where are we now?"

J: "We need to go back to the map, the FD framework, which is a grand abstraction of the essentials of sustained high performance. How the flywheel of sustained high performance of the few works against the flywheel of common wisdom.

We are looking at the cardinal directions for the journey, from the centre, and the principles involved. We started with people and positions because what we see depends on where we stand. To fix our positions we need some kind of reference points, the sun, moon, the stars or a compass or a GPS for a terrestrial journey. The same principles hold good for the other journey that we are discussing. The fixed position is our own centre, the home position, that we have the potential to improve continually. Having done that, we turn our attention to the NW quadrant of the FD framework, the potential. The SE is about performance and the gap between potential and performance which sets the direction for the journey of continual improvement, the process of recession-proofing."

M: "What about NE and SW?"

J: "It is the conflict between what we know and we need to know to go ahead with the journey. If NE is the garbage in us, SW is about developing a technology to convert it into organic manure."

M: "I certainly need another cup of coffee."

J: "I need one of those 'injurious to health' poison sticks. Let us contribute to the GDP and ward off the recession to some extent."

M: "I am afraid that I will have to take a break from this dialogue. I have an interesting offer which I am accepting."

J: "Congrats on recession-proofing for another stretch of the journey. We can continue the dialogue through mails.

We need to take a closer look at the architecture at the core."

Some more FAQs

J and M were cafe-hopping in Bangalore across several days. Between coffee, lunch, clouds of smoke, coffee again and beer, the dialogue continues:

M: "How do I make my business, recession proof? Is there a secret?" (J had borrowed the CD of *The Secret* from M, the previous day)

J: "Correction, how do I make myself recession proof? The secret is that there is no secret. It is pretty obvious. For most of us the code is to fail, go up and come down, boom and bust, birth and death, big bang and big crunch. They test the code and confirm that the code holds good and wait for their incentives, stock options and Nobels. The more elaborate and grandiose the project, the more is the competitive advantage. The economics of scale is in your favour."

M. "I saw it coming every time, on all six jobs spanning a career of nearly two decades. Got out in the nick of time when the downturn hadn't begun. This is one good thing about the managerial career. A doctor or the captain of a ship would be sued for dereliction of responsibility. You seem to have done quite the opposite; you were stuck in your last job for 24 years!"

J: "Your planning horizon was 3 years for your business and 15 years for your career. Mine was 40+ years, since I decided to be a Facilitator. I did not differentiate between my career horizon and my personal one. I think I have enough steam left to go on for more than the remaining 13 years. I have retired but not retired from work, that would be another kind of suicide. So if you want to recession-proof yourself you need to visualise your career over a longer planning horizon. If you want to recession-proof your business, the minimum planning horizon should be 10-14 years, covering a boom and bust, a complete cycle. In addition, you need to get rid of all those codes they planted in you over the years, at home, in the church, at school/college and by the democrats and republicans; all taken together, over time, at least since the industrial revolution."

M: "That is indeed a tall order. I don't have that kind of patience, period."

J: "I think we are stuck here. But anyway, since you have time on your side, have recession-proofed yourself for another two years; let us go ahead with the dialogue. It is better than going back to the same TV channels where they spread more gloom about the future of free markets and governments rushing in to bail out the pyramids. We are turning pro governance overnight!"

M: "Where do we begin?"

J: "Let us begin from the beginning; *First Things First* (Stephen Covey, A. Roger Merrill and Rebecca R. Merrill). Where are we now?"

M: "We have moved down from the heights of irrational exuberance to the depths of depression? Change is the only constant. It is like a roller coaster, a giant wheel for grown ups."

J: "Mind your language! It shows your code. In that case, changelessness also is a constant. Better debug your code for change and making a difference to MAKING IMPROVEMENTS AND MAKING CONTINUAL IMPROVEMENTs if you really want to recession-proof yourself and your business. You are no better than your code, your maps and tools."

M: "So where do we begin, with the clock or the compass?"

J: "We go back to principles, always the compass first not the clock. They don't change like you change into casuals and formals depending on the context.

Making a difference, my foot . . . We need better maps for the journey ahead, a language of performance and improvement."

M: "Yet another model?"

J: "Not another model, a map of principles that hold good for all the journeys of improvement, terrestrial, mental and/or spiritual, whatever kind of journey that is, that lies ahead."

M: "Tell me more."

J: "Let us look at the Ps Map."

M: "The 4 Ps, 7 Ps? Product, price, promotion, place, people, process . . ."

J: "All those Ps together will not recession-proof you or your business. But they will be useful when the missing Ps are taken care of, like the PHYSICIST from PHYSICS.

Come back to the map and assume that you are the traveller. What will be the first step, before the first step, to any journey? For seventeen years, I have been asking this question to mostly students of business, managers or businessmen and I am yet to get the right answer within a minute. Probably this was the first time they were confronted with it. Most of them position products and organisations, yet seldom apply the same logic to their careers/ personal lives."

J: "So after Principles, the next two Ps are PEOPLE and their POSITIONS. The first step on the journey is to answer the question— Where am I now? Where are we now? Fixing our lighthouse position, the invariant one, and then the variant positions in the direction of the journey and keep reflecting on the course in relation to the lighthouse position."

M: "Let us take a P break?"

J: "What is that?"

Joan meets Devassia—Stages of man

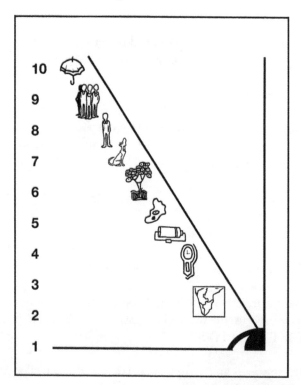

"In my father's house, there are many rooms,"—John 14:2

Or there are many levels, the bare minimum of which need to be ten as the figure shows. At times we call them the logic gates or gates to learning.

Joan Erikson and P.C. Devassia in a tete a tete:

PCD: "Congrats Joan, both you and Erik were born in 1902, but you outlived him by three years and added one more stage to his eight though I would not fully agree with you there. I lived to be a 100 and six months and gave up my life because I had completed my work on earth. The last six months were my preparation to quit. I would not call it old age. What strikes me most about the two of you was that Erik was very open in acknowledging your contributions to his work and admitting that it was impossible to separate who did what. You certainly will continue to be exceptional examples of family dynamics and professional growth."

JE: "You don't agree with our nine stages of man."

PCD: "I decided what to do with my life when I was nine and continued doing it for 91 years. So it is not the chronological age that matters, but whether you take a position in life as to the meaning and purpose of your life. Some might do this in their mid life and many will never even pass through the first of the ten transformative gates, from the human animal to the human. Most people are dead in their 30s and 40s though they manifest some symptoms of life, going by the laws of motion. Another problem is time in the West is perceived as linear. For us a 6,000-year-old story is as much in the present as it is 6,000 years in the future. We have a different way of perceiving time."

JE: "What would you propose in place of our nine stages of life?"

PCD: "We resorted to an ingenious way of crafting stories to carry content. Our philosophy is packaged into stories and transmitted through generations and they are perennial. We have two of the all-time best storytellers, Valmiki and Vyasa. Valmiki gave us the *Ramayana* and Vyasa the *Mahabharata*. Between the two stories, the stages of man are elaborated. The two stories are complementary to each other; the first one is more about family dynamics and the second one has a global canvas."

JE: "Can you explain the stages of man using these stories?"

PCD: "Let us take the character of Ravana in the *Ramayana*. Valmiki draws upon his own life prior to his transformation to create this character. Ravana has ten heads, is very accomplished and is an immortal, a boon he received for the austerities he practised for 10,000 years. The ten heads symbolise ten stages, avatars, of evolutionary growth. Yet he is considered a primitive, prakrit. He is juxtaposed against the protagonist Rama, the icon of the transformed man. He has the qualities of a catalyst. In his presence Ahalya, a petrified woman, is transformed into her completeness. Though he has passed through many of the gates of transformation he fails to do justice to his wife.

Ravana despite all his powers falls to win over Sita. Rama recovers Sita from captivity and Ravana is killed. Ravana is our man of the day."

JE: "I am more curious about what happened to Sita."

PCD: "That part of the story needs a re-telling in our context. We had female philosophers, like Gargi and Maitreyi, but no female versions of Valmiki or Vyasa. In *The Palace of Illusions* Chitra Banerjee Divakaruni re-tells the story of Panchali, the central female character of the *Mahabharata*, from a feminine perspective."

JE: "Despite all this noise and silence, the feminine will prevail. Men are such empty drums devoid of their feminine. May be I will work on gender intelligence in my next lifetime."

PCD: "It is easier for a camel to go through the eye of a needle, than for a rich man to enter into the kingdom of God."

JE: "The camel is in a better position."

A user manual to the self

"Dad"

"Yes, Johnny?"

"My PC is not working."

"Look up the user manual."

"Dad"

"Yes, Johnny?"

"The UPS is not working."

"Look up the user manual."

"Dad"

"Yes, Johnny?"

"I can't figure this out. Where is my user manual?"

"Ask Panditji." (Panditji is the neighbourhood astrologer and dad a professor of Strategic Human Resource Management in an Ivy League b-school)

Machines and gadgets come accompanied by a user manual. But we do not come across a user manual for the most sophisticated system that we own and use—the self. We use it in very different ways and pay very heavily for our ignorance of the design of the system.

There must be some principles that one cannot do without for achieving better outcomes. Self is the system through which we 'see', create meaning and make choices. The choices decide whether our actions lead to improvement or otherwise.

With more and more options available to each one of us, the opportunity could as well be a threat. How the interface is aligned will decide whether it will lead to greater good or havoc.

CHAPTER 3

The First Discipline Framework

"Give me a place to stand and with a lever I will move the whole world."—Archimedes

Going home

This is not about the home on a website or the physical home where we rest our bodies. So where is home?

6y4 ii3q qn320w3—I got this gibberish when I shifted from my home position on the keyboard, F and J where I rest my index fingers. When I move away from my home position, this is the result that I get. When I am at home on the keyboard I make sense otherwise I make nonsense. I can use appropriate levers and leverage to move the whole world; improve. If I am not at home, positioned, I create waste, work very hard, feel stressed by the work, burn myself faster and hurt myself and others in different ways. Work, anyway, is not fun.

Home is the only place from which I can move the world. The real journey begins here.

The home position

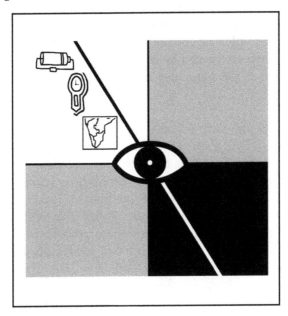

Even if we are homeless, we have homes on web sites. When we go off course, we can refer back to home and continue to navigate. We understand reality through our tools. It is a long time since I have used a pen or pencil or paper. I spend most of my working time in front of the monitor and the PC is my most used tool. When we were hunting and gathering, we would have used more of our hands and feet. With settled agriculture, we became more attached to a physical location and so did our mental maps of the world. The fishermen are quite different. On the high seas they don't have the kind of stability that we on land take for granted. Their mental models are different from that of the farmer. They use the compass or GPS since it is much more disastrous if they cannot locate their position/s. They could drift off and never return home.

When we got 'educated', we became language and 'English-centric', says Wanderer, my friend from a social network which was home to some of this writing. It took years to realise what he meant by being English-centric. Wanderer adds, "Your language is Inglish, not English." I admit. He is senior to me and has wandered around far more than any of us.

The paradigms are changing as HTML text, the visual and multi-modal replace text as we used to know it. One is lucky if we manage to retain a

Wiki page for a lifetimes work. Technology helps one see reality as it unfolds. Reading gives way to browsing and if one wants to capture the flea-span attention of the reader, one has to use more of the visual, and Youtube it. Yet, the deep structures influence comprehension of reality and to connect across divergences and barriers created by language and tools we need a 'Babel fish' which would reduce the noise and help navigate the semantic or semiotic swamps.

During our times we have become less earthbound in our internal and external horizons. We cover much more distance in a day than ever before, be at home and remain connected in real time across the planet. Perspectives change with the position. Visibility is much more from the top of the mountain, but the details get blurred. Products and solutions are designed and positioned to meet the global and local requirements of users. Personal and organisational positioning precedes and influences the process. A critical mass of catalytic material, individuals and organisations are a transformational imperative. Positioning is about those life changing decisions, the raison d'être, like choosing a vocation and deciding to be the best in that vocation, willing to sacrifice one's life for it, work against all odds, make great sacrifices for a cause.

The child in the womb is blissfully unaware of its position. The terrorist is firm in his position that the other deserves death. The negotiator takes the middle ground (yes and no, you and me). The catalysts take the fourth position, the home position or the lighthouse position where they are at home and anchored. Work transforms to living, expression of one's self. Here is the birth of the fully functional self, the beginning of conscious evolution characterised by dynamic mental maps, flow, synchronicity and continual renewal. Now, one can fix the direction of the journey (continual improvement), connect the home position to the variant position (reflect) and be certain that one is on course. Evolutionary growth and true community is in emergence.

When we are confronted by problems with our tools, we go back to the design or the user manual. Our tools have become very refined, yet the problems continue to outpace them. Without an understanding of the basic design it is quite possible that we become slaves to our own tools. Nature has a design, a deep structure, which we have to live with. We continue to pay a price for our ignorance of the basic design. Our designs are but improvisations of bits and bytes of the basic design. Imagine billions of people continuing with a flat earth world view and the reality we collectively create! While we have 'progressed' we have also 'regressed' in our connectedness with nature. Deep down, we still hold on to the flat earth static models. Better maps would facilitate faster and sustained improvements by leveraging technology and markets which work in real time and help us make more intelligent use of these levers with lesser damage.

We have very sophisticated tools for spatial navigation, ranging from the compass/GPS to satellites and communication systems. We have mapped our immediate environs with greater and greater precision and managed to connect machines to communicate with each other across the planet in real time. For the first time we see the planet in real time. Though machines communicate with each other we do not do it as well. The man-machine interface is still a grey area that slows down the common journey. A real time evolutionary framework of wholeness is one of the requirements to bridge the divides and disconnects.

The window to the self—A thought experiment

Return to the centre and the new beginning: Imagine yourself at the centre of a perfect sheet of rubber being stretched in the conflict between the old and the new, the ideal and the operational. Being a perfect sheet of rubber it does not get torn but stretches perfectly. The centre of the sheet remains at the centre, undisturbed

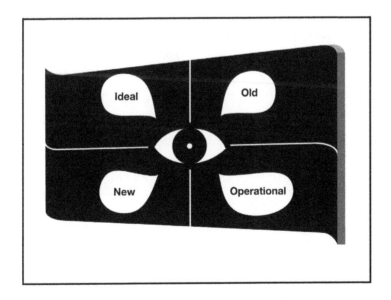

Now imagine the sheet being transformed into a perfect football. What happens to the centre? The centre shifts to the centre of the football and the football is kicked around in the world cup with no timelines. It is a perfect football. Nothing happens to the centre. It remains at the centre absolutely centred, motionless and at peace. Some time during the process of being kicked around, the football becomes aware of what is going on. Instead of being chased around it decides to chase the players!

Imagine your own self, the conflicts and the process of becoming anchored, taking the lighthouse position and the beginning of the journey of sustained continuous improvement.

Infographics—return to the centre

Getting started: I have a new DP, dialogue partner. We have decided to meet at the Ashoka Pillar in Bangalore. The pillar is a replica of the one at Sarnath (250 BC). My DP is new to Bangalore and spent quite a long time finding me.

"I had a problem with my GPS."

"Thank god you know that you have a problem with your GPS. Most people think they don't have a problem with their GPS."

"What do you mean?"

"What is the first thing we need to know if we want to reach our destination? Usually, we get a wide set of answers except THE FIRST, which is: Where am I now."

"So where are we now?"

"We may have to ask more questions before we come to the answer. When were you born?"

"dd.mm.yyyy"

"That was the birth of your body. You didn't have anything much to do with it and you are not your 60 kgs."

"Are you suggesting that I am yet to be born?"

"WE are yet to be born. How can I be born if WE, the species, is yet to be born?"

Birth of self and community self

We were not born when we were born since physical birth is not synonymous with the birth of the self.

The system at birth is comparable to the bullet that leaves the barrel of a gun. The bullet is helpless to influence its trajectory. Systems that we design do not go beyond this level, though the duration could be much longer.

Self-regulation is the differentiator to qualify to be a higher level system, evolving to become aware of the position, direction and regulating itself to influence the outcome, choosing the course to the potential of the design.

The key words are birth of self, position, direction, reflection and self-regulation.

Another question: what are our basic needs?

We have already re-visited Maslow; meaning/spiritual/whatever . . . For those who commit suicide, life is no more meaningful, not worth the trouble. If life is meaningful, then food has meaning—to keep the body and soul together.

Soul is the unifying principle—that which connects, the glue, gives meaning, spirit. We haven't really started. We are already getting mired in the semantic swamp. The semantic swamp contributes to global warming, cutting down more trees and creates more intellectual poverty rights.

Symbols make it easier than all the text and discourses.

The philosophy and the maths are very simple, the new maths or the very old, I don't know:

$0, 1, 2, 3, \Pi$

Where

0 = nothing

1 = everything

2 = duality, the linear, static, partial truth

3 = connecting, the linear is transformed

Π = synergy, whole > the sum of parts, dynamic, continual, real time, unending, quality of being connected with the centre and the periphery (the perfect football). When the setting is right, the intent is expressed, the seed turns into the tree, caterpillar to the butterfly and the bullet becomes aware of itself, takes birth to eternity. The journey begins here, that of transformation.

"Well-nigh two thousand years and not a single new god,"—Nietzsche.

We see the light at the end of the tunnel and walk out of the dark hole, the prison that we built for our SELVES.

Oneness is the quality of the whole—the child in the womb is one with the mother and at birth is confronted by the separation, a perceived duality which is the quality of two, a linear world of many, day and night, good or bad, true or false, yes or no; the domain of problems.

The prodigal son revolts and eventually reconciles. The self evolves to resolve the contradictions, duality and recognise the connectedness—oneness. This is not a return in the sense of going back since the self has moved to a higher level in terms of growth and maturity from the level of yes or no, true or false to the level of yes and no, true and false, good and bad. This is the quality of three: trinity, the third position from which agreement, improvement and solutions are possible; the shift from the static and linear to the dynamic and static.

Intelligent choices and conscious evolution follow.

So where are we now?

Other lesser FAQs

Which is true north, the direction for the journey?

How do WE make sure that WE are on the path?

Do we have a map of every-THING, to make it easier and fool proof?

Nothing to Everything

Design of the learning engine

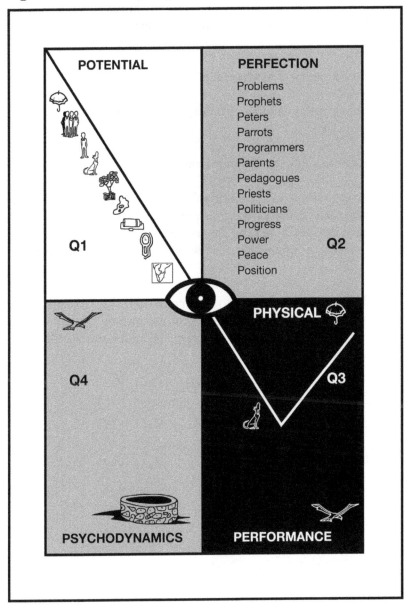

J: "The learning engine (LE) is any system that continually improves on its previous best performance."

S: "Am I one?"

J: "You can be one. It involves taking the (home) position that you are one, knowing what it means to be one. In the same way if a team, an organisation or a community decides to be one, it certainly qualifies to be a LE."

S: "Besides taking position what more does it involve?"

J: "It involves understanding the design and matching the performance with the design."

S: "Let us get to know the design in detail."

J: "Windows takes us to the world of the digital. This window to the self has four panes giving us the four perspectives from the centre. It took over three decades to see the connection with the four lions around the centre which communicates the essence of the four-fold view of the wheel of dharma."

J: "Quadrants, the four panes of the window, Q1, Q2, Q3 and Q4 of the LE are analogous to the four wheels of the car and the eye, the centre, the anchor, home position or whatever—a non-controversial reference point for metrics.

The four quadrants are also directional. Thus:

Q1: North West

Q4: South West

Q2: North East

Q3: South East"

S: "Who is the driver?"

J: "Us, depending on whoever identifies with the system. Q1 and Q4 are internal to the observer, driver/s of the LE. Q2 and Q3 are external to the observer. Q3 is the physical world."

J: "At the centre, where the four quadrants meet, imagine a lighthouse with nine levels. When you climb to the top you get the eagle's perspective, see everything and have a map of everything.

Level 1 has all the maps of the physical/geographical world; Level 2 maps of all the simple machines similar to the clock; Level 3 the maps of advanced machines with self-regulation; Level 4 the maps of the unicellular world; Level 5 that of the world of plants; Level 6 that of all the animals; Level 7 the maps of the individual human; Level 8 that of the organisational; and Level 9 that of all accumulated learning, meta-systems—religion, science, philosophy and so on."

A map of everything

From the top of the lighthouse, we can see where we were, prior to the climb, at the end of the line going up (or down) from the level of animals in quadrant SE. Now, one knows the lighthouse position (invariant) and the ship's position (variant).

The direction for the journey can now be set, the compass function, towards bridging the gap between potential and performance. Had there been no gap, we would have had a straight line in quadrant SE, a mirror image of NW. The gap is the waste, unrealised potential, road not travelled, blue ocean space; the domain of metrics, inputs for course correction, to make sure that the journey is one of improvement rather than speeding towards disaster.

SW is about learning and renewal—the process, improvement and revision of mental models to maps.

Quadrant NW is the external social system, history, barriers to transcend, opportunities which conflict with SW in terms of the challenges to learning and improvement.

Perfection, Problems—every single time is a time of crisis, a crisis of the spirit, of the time taking its birth, arising from resisting the perfection in us, not a crisis or a problem when we look at it from the invariant position, but the greatest opportunity of the time.

Prophets, Peters, Parrots—Christ's vision was the foundation for the church and Peter the institution builder. Sans vision, institutions become empty drums. In the age of the common Buddha, vision and action go hand in hand. Pyramids and hierarchies collapse. Parroting, rote learning, helps pass on accumulated learning, but is not sufficient to lead to improvement.

Programmers, Parents, Pedagogues, Priests, Politicians—even children are trained/programmed to be terrorists; Parroting. Why not have programming for sustained improvements. The major programming influences—family, religion and politics groom to conform. It is for the individual to discern between the chaff and the grain in his journey of improvement.

Progress—Many a measure of progress fails to capture net improvements in realising the unrealised potential of the human. What we might think of as progress may not be an improvement as suggested in quadrant SW. We might believe ourselves to be above the level of animals as a class, but when it comes to realising potential we fall below them.

Power, Peace—Aggression begets aggression. Authentic power follows from facilitating others to discover their power, voice, potential, anchoring and connecting to peace within for peace outside.

Process—The focus on events, outcomes and results needs to go hand in hand with process dimensions. The product is in the process. If output and results do not meet expectations and standards, revisit the process.

Position—Taking a position calls for multiple perspectives, variant and invariant, the lighthouse position vs. the positions that the ship takes on its course.

The core at the centre is the engine and the four quadrants, the wheels. The learning engine is capable of continually improving on its own performance against all odds, creating invincibility.

Continual renewal—Continual learning is the path to continual renewal. Nature is in a process of continual renewal but for the ecological footprints of human interventions. It takes more than a year for nature to renew what we consume in a year and some damage is irreparable.

Learning improves our mental models. The frog in the well forms a model of the world. The eagle on the tree has a different model. When the frog is taken out by the eagle and brought back into the well these two merge together to form a map of the world. The world has not changed, but the models of the world have changed. We too had a flat earth model in the not too distant past. With better technology and tools these models have given way to maps with increasing precision. Though maps of the physical world have become more precise, the mental models that went with them are not easily discarded.

The eagle represents the big picture and the frog the details. Both are connected just as the Hubble telescope sends us pictures from outer space and the Femtoscope helps us see the smallest of the small. The eagle represents the global and the frog the local, which are but different perspectives of the whole. In a connected world being GLOCAL is an imperative. So is the imperative of continual learning, leading to continual renewal. We are frogs in the well of nature.

The map attenuates variety in sufficient measure to reveal what is concealed. It facilitates positioning, fixing direction and self-correction for the process of continual renewal and improvement at different levels—individual, institutions, communities and community. We know where to hang our different hats as practitioners of various disciplines, 'social programmers'— parents, pedagogues, priests and politicians. We can SEE and SHOW (the visual has the highest bandwidth) how everything, living, non-living, internal and external, observer and observed are ONE; a continuum in process and evolving. It points to the blue ocean space, the un-trodden path to our evolutionary potential. The observer could be the individual, a group, an organisation or the species.

Metrics, measurement, of true progress becomes possible.

NW is a map of the ideal, the deep structure, the conceptual, pure potential, design and the world of ideas. The order, hierarchy, increasing complexity and potential with each level, alignment and connectedness need be re-'cognised' to understand the performance issues in the external world mapped in the bottom right quadrant, SE.

The wheels must be in alignment for the car to move on. There exists a perennial conflict (resistance to change) between quadrants NW and SE, ideal and the operational; between internal self and the external social system, quadrants SW and NE. To manage is to create, sustain and continually improve the alignment so that the car is on course, feeding on its fuel.

What makes the human unique as a class of systems is the potential to improve. There is 'no' gap between potential and performance up to the level of animals (see quadrant SW).

The gap begins after the level of animals. The gap can also be seen as the waste in the system, the unrealised potential, the root cause of problems. In terms of potential vs. performance, the human is sub-animal.

Corresponding to the total potential/performance gap, there exists a gap in every one of us which forms the personal sphere for improvement, which triggers the question: What is my potential and my performance?

Quadrant NW represents the ideal, perfect, conceptual, pure potential, internal to the self and in perfect alignment at all levels starting from the maps to meta-systems (represented by the umbrella).

Quadrant SE represents the physical world, measurement, performance. Mirrors NW up to the level of animals. The knowledge gap is the major reason for the gap. There will always be a gap, but it is possible to narrow the gap and bring about sustained and continual improvements.

Quadrant SW is internal to the self and NE represents the external social system. While learning is a prerequisite to improvement, history and habits nurture conformity. This is both a challenge and an opportunity. The self could be the individual, team, organisational or community self. Complexity increases with levels.

The map facilitates positioning, fixing the direction of the journey and measurement of progress. It is possible to visualise the nature of the journey as an ongoing process of continual improvement and renewal.

"A journey of a thousand miles begins with a single step," said Confucius. To take that first step we need to know where our position is and the direction in which to take that step, to be on course.

The potential performance gap is illustrated by life expectancy vs. longevity of exceptional people. Life expectancy in developed countries is around 75, which is an indication of performance. Potential is reflected in the exceptions, people living beyond 100. The gap or the waste in terms of unrealised potential is 25 years.

Life expectancy is not the only aspect to be taken into account. There are exceptions who achieve much more than average people in shorter life spans and those who continue to be much more productive in their second careers than in their first.

We need to visualise human potential if we are to realise it. On a global scale, the aggregate waste is astounding. The estimation has to be on multiple factors to illustrate the issue better. A corporate would attempt to look at the issue from many different perspectives, in terms of market potential vs. performance or the human potential vs. performance. The same can be attempted at different levels—individuals, institutions, communities, nations and so on.

The scope for improvement is defined by current performance against the potential of the system. Improvement is constrained by gaps in understanding/internal competencies that define the learning requirements to realise such improvements. The roadmap and metrics to narrow the gap between potential and performance emerges.

When breakdowns are pervasive, it is time to go back to the design. We have enough reasons—poverty, recession, illness, crime, suicides, terrorism and the climate challenge—to go back to the basic design, the template/s of nature, the system of systems.

The unknown is a rabid dog without its master. When it finds the master it turns into his/her most faithful ally. It is the submerged portion of the iceberg of our self, personal and collective. The further away we move from the basic design, and it remains unknown and unconnected, the scale and complexity of our challenges assume gargantuan proportions.

On potential and performance

Quadrant 3 is the performance quadrant. In an ideal situation we would have had a straight line beginning from the centre and going to the opposite corner. This is the fall of man which we often view, as 'Progress'. One can now see the gap between potential and performance—the waste in the system, the unrealised potential, the root cause of all breakdowns.

To illustrate at the personal level, what is the potential vs. performance of the body?

I got to know P.C. Devassia when he was 75 years old. My relationship with him continued till he died at the age of 100 years, 6 months and 15 days. Life expectancy in the context in which he lived is 74 years. There is a gap of 26 years when one compares his performance against what is considered to be normal. He was abnormal in a positive sense because he achieved many times more than the normal individual and was healthy and cheerful till the very last. But for an accident towards the end, he never had to go to the doctor or take medicines. Other than the last few weeks, he continued to work.

Why is it that there is such variance? If we visualise a future society with 100 years as the norm, there is a waste of 25-odd years at present. Why do such variances occur and how do you explain the gap between potential and performance?

The problem is not with the potential of the body or the design, but with our understanding of the design. The first problem is the knowledge hole, much more serious than the ozone hole! Human potential is something like an iceberg: We see only a small part of it. What is hidden is much more than what is revealed, far beyond all that is known to us, beyond all those who are in the *Guinness Book*. Nothing about the past gives us any clues to this unrealised potential other than perhaps the myths. There is plenty of room for miracles to happen because a miracle is something that is unexplainable by the known laws of nature. What we know of nature is so fragmented that it does more harm than good and precedence will not take us to Mars.

The model is about understanding the design in nature. The second step is to use this design to check whether performance matches the design. It doesn't. The gap between potential and performance as shown in Q3 in the framework, helps us visualise this gap. How do we connect to that potential in us that is hidden; connecting to an infinite source of power? The moment of truth! The alignment needs be right for the car to move. The known and the unknown, conscious and the unconscious, are to be in alignment if the full potential is to emerge, if not they work at loggerheads. The unknown is our enemy which fights/plots against our own selves. Dreams and myths offer a bridge to the unconscious. During the time of Hippocrates, the patients had to dream that they were healed prior to the physician commencing his medication.

In Quadrant 3, the potential performance gap begins from the level of animals. What we see as a rise in the line from the diagonal is a fall, the great fall of man turning himself into the sub-animal despite our 'progress'. For animals there is hardly any gap between potential and performance, but from the level of the human there exists this gap. The human is the only species that can improve itself; the unique differentiator of humanness. And when we don't improve as a species, we turn sub-animal. It is not that we don't want to improve, but there has to be a method by which we differentiate between real improvements and pseudo achievements.

Q3 is the physical world, the tangible and material while Q2 deals with the external world; the accumulated wisdom or ignorance of the social system which influences the self and the barriers created by the external world in realising one's higher potential.

If you think about it, there are four different worlds—the ecosystem people, farming communities, the industrial world and a post-modern knowledge community in the making. There are lessons to be integrated from all the four worlds to create a more desirable future. The first world lives or used to live in harmony with nature, living off nature without hurting sustainability. Agriculture in the developed world has become industrialised. Farming communities in developing countries, though not industrialised to the same extent, are compelled to compete with industrialised agriculture. Industrialisation brought about major shifts in the way we think because the tools we use influence our thinking and leads to behavioural modifications. With the emergence of connectivity and communications, paving the way for the emergence of a global community, the possibility of another paradigm shift is emerging.

However, the dominant thinking, the mental models of our opinion makers—politicians, economists, engineers, medical professionals and others—essentially follows the machine logic.

It is not an unfounded fear that in some distant future robots or artificial intelligence will take over humans. In a sense, it has already happened since we are driven by machine logic—a product of industrialisation—as our prevalent paradigm, the internal map. Are we turning into Pavlov's dogs?

Machine logic is focused on entropy. No machine can regenerate itself, reproduce itself or make a copy of itself; not yet at least. It is not a self regulating system, though advanced machines have some limited capacities to self regulate.

Economists visualise the economy as an engine and the allopath sees the body as a machine. The biologist has a better model guided by bio-logic, in stark contrast to machine logic. Bio-logic is about creating order, increasing self regulation as we move up through the different classes of beings. That humans do not often self regulate does not mean that there is no potential. Entrenched habits block this potential from emerging and conscious choice is a pre-requisite to self regulation. The cell, the basic unit of life, is negentropic with increasing order and evolution. Two hundred years since Darwin, the biologist does not influence our thinking to the extent that other more fashionable professions do—the engineers, managers, economists or those in the medical profession. These are essentially derived disciplines, emerging out of our progress in knowledge and there will always be a lag between new understanding and such understanding influencing mainstream thinking. One has to take position against the limits of mainstream thinking, the burden of normality, if one has to move beyond the average; a perceived normality rather than true normality.

The cardinal illness is a thought disorder and other problems are ones derived from this fundamental distortion; the original sin, perhaps.

Quadrant 2, more Ps

Q2 comes between the blocks/barriers to transcend/narrow the gap between potential (Q1) and performance (Q3).

Nature is perfect, beyond improvement. Nurture follows from history, institutions, assumptions, habits and positions. All these together create the knowledge hole, barriers to realising the unrealised but realisable potential, personal and collective. This is the learning imperative, the syllabus for graduation from the school of life.

Being from and of nature we are complete and whole (by design), but we seldom take such a position. We take the position that we are incomplete, sinners and wait for the second coming of the prophet, to be redeemed.

What we see depends on where we stand—our position. The individual, organisation, community or society at large could be positioned for improvement or otherwise. Some take the informed choice and go by the design and others take the road by default. The two options are by design or by destiny and the answers could be 'yes', 'no' and 'yes and no'. There is enough room for dialogue.

Positioning is the first step to progress or continuous improvement. Clashes arise from the differing positions and finding common ground is essential to bring in peace. Power comes in between, sometimes genuine and authentic and at other times distorted arising from the primary distortion in the meaning of power. (Gandhi vs. Hitler)

Nature is always in a process of continual renewal. The body is in the process of continual renewal, which depends on what we pay attention to. Pay attention to entropy and decay is the result. From completeness arises completeness, growth from acceptance, being to becoming.

Programming—socialisation—of the individual thorough institutions of politics, religion (priests), education (pedagogues) and parents influences progress. Whether it's for better or worse depends on the position one takes.

Peters and Parrots, the effectiveness would depend on the vision with which they are driven. Rote learning is parroting, not real. Real learning leads to real improvements. Sometimes parroting helps. Without parroting we wouldn't have any myths, folklore or culture. We would have lost our roots and become impoverished.

Problems can be perceived as problems or as opportunities. Complexity is a challenge to those who enjoy it and a puzzle for those who are perplexed by it. The solution is that focus would accelerate progress and the opposite to compounding of the problem.

Quadrant 4 addressing the learning imperative

Earlier in this chapter we came across the story of the eagle and the frog(s) in the well. We have been collecting these stories since 1990. Initially everyone connects to it in their own way. Some identify with the eagle and others with the frog and the fear of death.

Not many though, identify with both the eagle and the frog—the big and the small; the telescope and the microscope; Hubble and the Femtoscope; global, local and the connections in between; how mental models are formed, revised and improved to mental maps; how best to continually learn and not to stop with any of the new maps; how the old world of the frog has collapsed and a new world is born; that we are all in that well—of Nature and that we will never see all of it, but can see much more now than earlier.

Continual learning is the path to continual renewal. Learning improves our mental models. The frog in the well forms a model of the world. The eagle on the tree has a different model. When the frog is taken out by the eagle and brought back into the well these two merge to form a map of the world. The world has not changed, but the models of the world have changed.

We were inhabitants of a flat land in a not too distant past. With better technology and tools these models have given way to maps with increasing precision. Though maps of the physical world have become more precise, the mental models that go with them are not easily discarded.

With a little facilitation everyone comes to share the common ground, the foundation for a Taj Mahal, an ashram or a lighthouse to be built. We have looked at the four wheels of the learning engine. We now need to move to the centre, the observer and driver of the learning engine and what drives her. It is also time to move away from orbiting, repetition, to join the dynamic conscious evolutionary spiral of continuous improvement /renewal.

Potential vs. performance

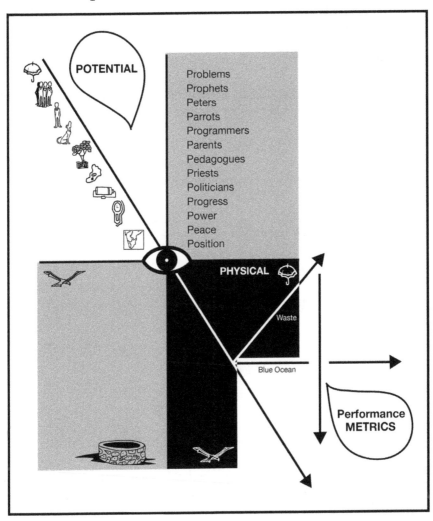

We take the two panes together so that the contrast helps us grasp the nature of the problem, like black vs. white a duality. We hold the view that a duality is nothing but a gate to learning.

Without black we cannot make sense of white. When we put it in black and white, we put only the black. White is the context. Meaning is contextual, relative, in comparison. The same goes for good and bad, true and false, war and peace. In the same way, if performance needs to be put in perspective we need to hold potential with performance and thus make sense.

The potential quadrant is of a conceptual nature whereas the performance quadrant is the tangible physical world as in the design of a car and the car itself.

In the potential quadrant:

- Ground zero is the meeting point between all quadrants, the position of the observer symbolised by the eye/ self

- Level of maps

- The level of the clock; all simple machines, a bullet leaving the barrel of a gun

- Systems with self regulation

- Level of the unicellular

- Level of the plant

- Level of the animal

- Level of the individual human

- Level of groups, organisations, community

- Level 10: Meta—accumulated and potential future knowledge

Potential is emergent from positioning and alignment with all levels. In the *Ramayana*, Ravana, the anti-hero, has ten heads (nine more heads within) corresponding to all the levels, yet he fails to win the heroine.

In the performance quadrant the gap between potential and performance begins from the level of the human. We can improve, but do not in aggregate terms. The blue ocean space is the collective unrealised potential of the system or in other words, the waste.

Metrics deals with the reduction in waste (pollution, illness, suicides), the measure of net improvements. Real progress is the reduction in the gap between potential and performance. The journey is in the right direction if continual renewal/improvement results.

Perfection vs. psychodynamics

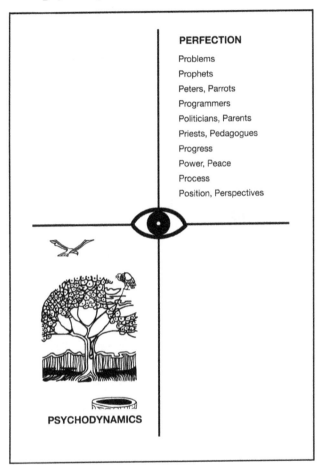

PERFECTION
Problems
Prophets
Peters, Parrots
Programmers
Politicians, Parents
Priests, Pedagogues
Progress
Power, Peace
Process
Position, Perspectives

PSYCHODYNAMICS

Nature is perfect by design. Our understanding is not and we refuse to accept our inherent perfection. This is the barrier to be transcended for the fuller expression of performance.

Psychodynamics is the interaction of conscious or unconscious mental or emotional processes influencing behaviour and attitudes. The story of the eagle and the frog(s) in the well explains the problem and also points to the solution space.

How best to continually learn and how does the old world of the frog collapse? How do the new frames come to sit on the older versions of our mindware? A new world is born. Yet we are all in that well—of Nature.

We will never see all of it, but we can see much more now than at any time in the past and 'there are miles to go before we sleep'.

Abstract to concrete: Imagination, intent, manifestation (IIM)

Nishtha asks, "JM, Where are you?"

Where am I NOW? I am 20 years into the journey with Nishtha

In Sanskrit, Nishtha means:

Assiduity, great and constant diligence and attention,

Firmness

Steadiness

Firm devotion

Application

Position

Discipline comes very close to it.

The question is about my position then; what is your 'nishtha' position, in space and time, now?

My profile gives my location as Bangalore. So the question is not about my physical location. It refers to my growing up as a person, my journey.

We need to ask more questions to give an answer to the question: Where am I? The first question on any journey, outside, inside, inside out, outside in, is: Where am I now? The second question is where do I want to go: the direction of the journey. The third is how do I make sure that I am on course: am I moving in the direction that I wanted to go and not speeding towards disaster. This is what a GPS or compass facilitates in our regular journeys.

So where am I now? I need to look back: Where was I?

1949: physical birth, bullet that left the barrel of the gun. A low level system without self regulation.

1981: takes the lighthouse position. The invariant one, the Facilitator. 'I am my position' (Peter M. Senge). I have not shifted from this position since. But I have other variant positions like the ship in relation to the lighthouse.

1981-90: I was busy making a map for the journey, a tool that helped me answer the three questions; 'The Map of Everything'.

1990 onwards: I am on the journey better 'equipped'.

We are on course, we believe. That leaves room for more questions:

Where were you before?

Where will you be in 2049, the centenary of the bullet?

Thank you, Nishtha. The universe must have conspired that we meet and you ask me this question.

The journey continues with nishtha—discipline.

The path

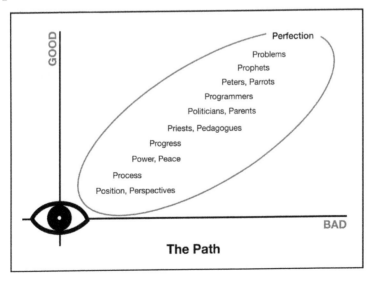

The Path

Nature is perfect, beyond improvement. Nurture follows from history, institutions, assumptions and habits—the knowledge hole.

Being from and of nature we too are complete and whole. From completeness arises completeness, being and becoming.

Why all the Ps?

It was nothing but synchronicity (or was it). It just fell in place. There are volumes written on each of the Ps, but the volumes will not give us the perspective that the visual gives.

Position, Align and Leverage

Sergey Bubka is my mental map for being positioned and ALIGNED for continual improvement. There is a visual of Sergey standing poised with the pole for the leap. We also have a female version in the making in Yelena Isinbayeva. Sergey is not just another sports person. He continues to do what he did on the field in other realms. The pole vaulter leverages the pole against the threshold to cross over and does it over and over to set new heights of performance. He is positioned and aligned to perform. Every pole vaulter does the same, but Bubka is the exception. So what goes into positioning, alignment and leveraging is much more than a question of a mechanical advantage. We take our cars to check for alignment. One could think of a similar service for people, organisations, communities and community (for the species).

The threshold level of performance is the benchmark against which positioning and alignment are tested and the proof of the pudding is in the eating—better and better results.

We can learn a lot from animals about positioning and alignment. It is natural to them. For us it is not natural, it is a matter of choice. Free will has its disadvantages too.

Matrix and matrix thinking: The very same wine, a slightly different bottle

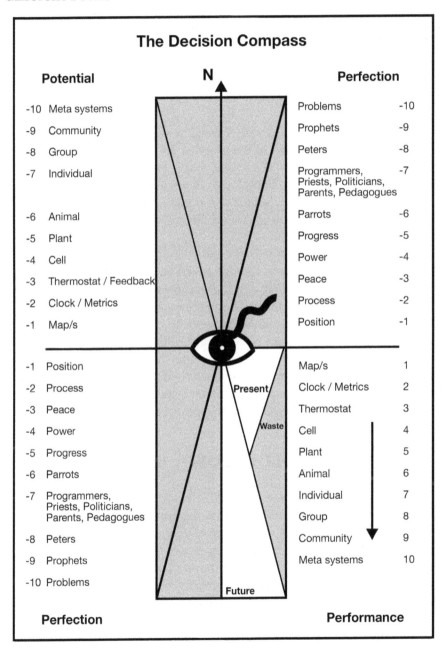

The sun rises in the east. The coin has two sides. Change is the only constant. Time runs out. Time is money. Death and illness are essential.

It is true or false, yes or no. It is destiny. Oh my God, what the Devil. Black and White.

I need 2,000-3,000 calories/day from food. Let us vote for change. Resources are limited and wants unlimited.

These little programs, cookies, were rejected by the matrix for incorrect logic. The programs reflect the logic of the programmer, the way they are internally organised. These programs were sent back to the recycling facility in Bangalore, India. They were Bangalored. Programs compete with each other. Every program, good or bad, has life and the life span varies with the quality of the logic. One with better logic prevails over the others. Such programs evolve and coalesce into maps.

For example, the map that says that it 'appears to us that the sun rises in the east' survives over the one that says the 'sun rises in the east'. Similarly, the one that says the 'coin has many sides' outlives the map that says 'the coin has two sides'. Resources are unlimited and needs limited takes precedence over the old paradigm of scarce resources and unlimited wants. The neo-logic was that the creative intelligence, the prime resource which transforms/catalyses the other resources, is unbounded. Unlimited wants were found to be derivatives of some of the primal survival drive distortions. The realisation was found to have survival value since it appealed to the selfish gene.

English > Inglish/ COBOL> COPOL (common purpose oriented language)

The logic for the new language was that the syntax of one's mother tongue went against the purpose of connecting—building bridges. It works like an empty parrot's cage or the classic golden mouse trap where rats were extinct for a very long time. The syntax of the mother tongue promoted imperialism (read, version Anglo-Saxon). With the emergence of the syntax of viewing, the syntax of text which promoted linearity became redundant.

The programs are stacked into levels, from maps to meta systems. Science is a meta system. So are art and religion. The matrix holds nothing to everything together.

The current version of the matrix has been in existence since 1990 (PME-0). A new skin has been added in the version PME-19, the only improvement in 19 years.

The project began with a classroom discussion in 1981. The case study was 'IT or MIT' (MIT, read Misinformation Technology). JJ had taken the position that the critical issue in IT is the issue of standardisation of the observer matrix. Since every observer sees with a different internal matrix, the resultant complexity would be unmanageable and IT would turn into MIT. Others stood for the remaining mostly hardcore technological issues. JJ took the position that what they see as hard is really soft and what they see as soft is hard. The entire class went against JJ's arguments. JJ stuck to his guns and walked out of the discussion. The project had begun.

We see what we pay attention to. What we choose to focus on is limited by the program which runs us and the positions we take, which most likely have nothing to do with the common good. We could be charging full steam towards our own destruction. This possibility no more exists with the emergence of the matrix, which has taken over the collective unconscious. Since the year of the matrix, 1990, 5,169 Neos have been trained in the matrix. Somewhere in between, the 100th monkey effect took over and the program now exists in everyone. The Neos are conscious of the existence of the matrix. Others are not. Some Neos work as teachers and healers, in food and livelihood security, software engineering and in medicine.

If you come across a Neo-doc, s/he is more likely to ask you in her/his diagnostic foray what your work is or whether what you do for a living is in sync with your purpose in life. The data shows that this is the MFQ (most frequently asked question) among Neos; what the purpose of the program is. Another MFQ is about the fabric/quality of community that supports our lives or about the quality of relationships outnumbering other questions on smoking, exercise or the number of calories that go into the system.

It took eight years for the matrix to fall in place. The cardinal frameworks had to pass the immortality test. The matrix went through innumerable tests to pass through all possible contexts past, present and future. The levels and hierarchy were to be assigned. For example, Christ is relatively more immortal than Shakespeare.

Successful centenarians work for over ninety years. Many of them have never consulted a doctor. For them work is self-expression. These people at the other end of the immortality continuum were studied in the formulation phase of the matrix. The single major challenge they faced to further extension of life spans was the absence of community, as most fellow travellers had taken the exit route. More than anything else, it was concluded that the quality of one's work decides health and life spans and quality follows from purpose. When one is ready to die for it, death will be afraid to approach one.

What am I suggesting here?

We are over deterministic in our assumptions and more often than not end up with the wrong diagnosis of our problems. We need a new way of looking, a set of new eyes if we want to craft a new vision.

In the *Matrix* trilogy, the Frenchman says, "It is my business to know." Yet he wants the eyes of the oracle

The key maker is a meta-programmer. His business is to architect the meta-program, the key to all programs; to make keys for all possible variety of programs.

The matrix is a perfectly balanced equation

It is our business to know because knowing is doing. Doing without knowing is not doing.

Black and White > Grey

Day and Night > Dusk and dawn, the in-between, gaps to fill, to connect.

We have a pair of eyes, but we see as one.

Ravana had 10 heads and 20 eyes. Still he could not see, avoid defeat or win the heart of Sita.

Dhritarashtra, the king in the *Mahabharata*, was blind inside and outside. The queen/advisors had eyes, but they opted to keep them shut or could not see the conflicts in the making. They were myopic, blinded by their selfishness.

One can have forty heads, levels, thinking hats/positions, take in 40 different/ variant perspectives and bring them together into one vision. Each level has infinite elements that form the class. It is for us to choose the specific ones relevant to our specific context/s. When one is ready to die for what one sees, others have no option but to come around to what such people see. Community is in the making when more and more agree to the immortality of the program. Ideas also follow the norm, survival of the fittest.

Nature is not impatient, in a hurry. For nature time does not run out.

Meanwhile, the material that makes the pearl accretes around the nucleus. The clusters that continually do this progress on the path, reducing the waste in the system, a self improving program. The only metrics being how much of the garbage, waste, has been recycled and transformed to organic manure. Non-physical garbage takes priority over the physical.

In comparison to the successful centenarians, most of us squander nearly half a century of our lives. The centenarians do not experience any recessions.

Multiply with the billions on earth to visualise the total waste, the unrealised potential. The list could be pretty long. Add poverty, illness, infant mortality, terror strikes, and wars in the name of peace . . .

Quality and quantity is the count. Quantity without quality is waste.

We can go on ad nauseum, but if you got it, you got it—explanations are redundant. If you didn't, ASK.

Is this fact or fiction? It is fact and fiction. Fiction is more powerful than fact. Myths live on, facts are forgotten. Leverage both facts and fiction; tell a future story.

Matrix thinking is thinking with nature, co-creating. There is no need to go out to fight any wars . . . a home improvement project. Let the noise die down.

Suggested reading:

Idealised Design—Russell L. Ackoff

CHAPTER 4

The Process: Sustained High Performance by Design

"The final strategy: Open the windows, close the gates, do a mother Teresa."—Ratsinger

Facts, fiction and metaphor

Are we guided by facts or fiction?

We are guided less by facts and more by myth, fiction and fantasy.

9/11 is a fact, not illusion; so are the war 1, war, 2 and war 3 now going on. We have democratised wars and conflicts, flattened them and dispersed them all over the planet.

Bear Stearns, Freddie Mac, Fannie Mae, Lehman Brothers, AIG—the pharaohs of financial pyramids walk away leaving their accumulated follies unleashed on the public. When the same happens to the farmers, suicide is the escape route for many.

Facts do not take hold of our minds as myth, fantasy and fiction do. Superman, Batman, Hulks, WWF, larger than life heroes/heroines, science fiction, star wars and particle accelerators are attempts at creating modern myths. We need more and more potent placebos, amnesiacs, analgesics and anti-BIOTICS—substitutes—to do away with the grim reality of life. Older myths still survive and we continue to be driven more and more by shadows and myths. We wish to forget facts or sweep them under the carpet.

In India, we have an ancient text called the *Bavishya Puranam*. Bavishya means future and puranam is an old epic story. I hope you see the twist. It is time for us to rely on myths to create a more desirable future. This is why we are compelled to talk in metaphors, since we are in the process of creating something which does not exist.

As technological bandwidth and connectivity increase, human bandwidth and connectivity decrease. I see this all around me, with my own children demanding more and more bandwidth and becoming less and less concerned about broader issues. I have begun to suspect that their jobs are creating an occupational hazard to them and society at large. The higher incidence of suicides in Bangalore, to me, is a bandwidth problem of the latter kind. So is the terrorist issue. The first step to the making of a terrorist is to narrow his bandwidth. The multitude of disciplines and the silos they create offer the best setting for the narrow bandwidths, which in turn chokes the channels creating more noise than communication. We need a meta discipline to connect the scientists, priests and the artist to transcend these barriers to communication and community since all the three are in the same business— explaining reality to lesser mortals like us.

The bandwidth problem is not exclusive to the younger generation. Institutions do pass through the process. The midlife crisis of the CEO is passed on to the organisation he heads, that of the politician to the country and that of the guru to the disciples.

I met Jo on the beach during my time with the fishermen. We continue to meet on the beach, less frequently now since he has moved to another shore. He is a Ph.D. in his area of expertise but you would not get these thoughts anywhere in his work or even in the classrooms when he teaches. There is a risk attached to wide bandwidth—one could be 'excommunicated'. He believes in many births/many lifetimes. He still has hopes of pulling me over to his position on birth and rebirth. I am tempted to do so when confounded by the recollection of childhood memories in our workshops. I am afraid that after the age of five there is a kind of growing down in the process of socialisation. Much later, one could reconnect with these memories and grow up. I am yet to make up my mind on whether to join his school or not, but I have gained a lot from his arguments.

Here is a summary of our many sessions on the beach since 1985:

Jo would watch the waves beating on the shore and would talk about the waves in the production of bio-mass in the sea and the consequent rise and fall in fish production, what it does to fishing, corresponding waves in farmers' produce on the land, the waves in life, business and markets. He taught me to see things as waves and cycles. He foresaw the present crisis in financial markets and the following economic slowdown, the big crunch in demand driven by the inability to connect to the voice of the masses across the planet. He has a pet theory on why Jesus recruited Peter as his CEO against our current paradigms of selection, recruitment, training and development. He challenged my b-school education: "If you have any competencies that you claim to have, go to the bottom of the pyramids and prove it rather than skimming the cream and stamping them with Ivy League labels." Christ chose Peter since he fit the bill in terms of his mental maps; maps that go with a fisherman. So the next time you go head hunting check their mental maps!

He stripped me of my notions of an internal flat land, which he told me is the inheritance of all land-based humans since the beginning of settled agriculture some 10,000 years ago. Prior to that, the fishermen and the people on the land had the same world view. Both were hunting and gathering.

Jo was born in a fisher family, used to go fishing with his father as a child, an outsider to the flat land, having lived on the coast and the sea for generations. A good fisherman has a different world view, one closer to reality than the humans on land. He is pushed to the brink much more than the farmer. He produces much more than the farmer yet he is poorer. He is seldom driven to suicide and the spirit of community is more alive in the ecosystem people who survive on common property resources.

He is the one who introduced me to the concept of digital/analogue bandwidths and the other bandwidth, of expectancies in human communication, and how the net result has not been any better. He has a very wide bandwidth which you would know only at a personal level. He would go on about how water is recycled on the planet, how everything is in a cycle or process, that there is nothing linear or 'straightforward' about nature and then take the quantum leap to conclude that we too pass through a higher order version of the process. If we want, we can break out of that giant wheel of birth and rebirth.

He challenged me with some insights from his many lifetimes.

Of the time he was in Egypt and Joseph's dream of the good years and bad years. How the natural cycles in primary production would hurt the farmers and how famines would result unless the state steps in to lend a helping hand when the cycles turn against the farmer and why, left to themselves, markets will fail the farmers. More so in the case of fishermen who have no property rights other than common property and open access to resources.

Of the time he was in Jerusalem and how Jesus had been reinvented over centuries to suit the bandwidth requirements of different times. Low bandwidth of practitioners leads to creation of silos and pyramids in disciplines, which kills community. And he would conclude with a sigh: "It is all about bandwidth, of people, technology and the interface."

The Process—Enhancing bandwidth

I was playing a game with 57 MBA students for two days. It went on from 9.00 am to 9.00 pm on day 1 and from 9.00 am to 6.15 pm on day 2.

Prior to the game I talked to a local politician to understand the business he is in—development of the locality.

I also talked to the students' professor to get some insights about these young men and women who are in the business of becoming businesspeople. Both the politician and the professor were exceptional people who will not fit in with our perceptions of the run of the mill in this category.

The game commenced with an assessment of their present position, globally and locally, in the context of the global meltdown and the situation of the locality.

Then the game with the students really began, simulating an organisation working together as a community for two days, with an open selection process to identify a group who would be offered premium placements on the basis of their mental maps. Then I checked their mental maps on many issues.

All of them had a map—as shown in the upper portion of the graphic—deeply ingrained in them. The code for failure: BOOMS AND BUSTS. With those maps they will build their towers of Babylon and will be Wall Street smart.

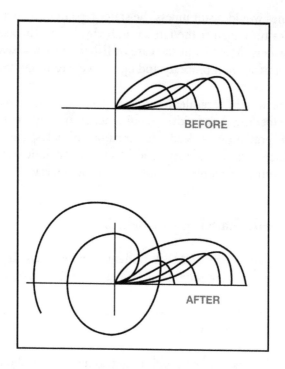

The upper portion of the graphic is about birth, maturity and death. The lower portion shows the shift to a dynamic one of continual improvement and renewal. Is such a shift possible?

The first set never goes beyond the level of a clock or a bullet leaving the barrel of the gun. The difference is only in the duration, time. The potential to self regulate or the potential to transform into a learning engine, a sustained high performance system, is not expressed. The claim to culture, civilisation, evolution and improvements are but empty boasts.

Why so?

Columbus reached America. He never wanted to go there. We are as good as our maps.

Can we have a better set of maps?

I told the students of the eagle's gift to the frog in the well. Between before and after, it is not the world that changed, but the frog's map of the world. This is all that we can do and that is good enough.

The problem is not with the world, but with our maps of the world.

We did quite a few other things, more stories, team learning, dialogues, Buddha's smile and discussed the First Discipline Framework.

They presented their understanding of the framework and told me of their dreams on the morning of the second day. They were surprised to look at their own process. All of them came up with evidence and data about the shifts, each contributing to the community learning process. We can indeed observe ourselves 24/7, the first step to continual improvement.

We positioned ourselves, fixed the direction of the journey and reflected on our improvements during the process. The shared space expanded as we moved along with the work. The map for a learning community was crafted and the process is on.

Simulating high performance: Defying gravity

This business strategy simulation happened at New University in Udayagiri, Tamil Nadu. There were 61 participants including three facilitators. The System of Profound Knowledge (Deming), helped us see how complex organisations work. Organisations guided by SPK will be more effective and successful. We demonstrated this using the First Discipline Framework. We told stories, about 15 of them. Every community needs to tell its own stories and recreate old stories. We reflected every now and then and the participants developed the game. And Harvard agrees with what we have been doing for twenty years.

The simulation itself: How do we fix true north (the true point)?

The business—transformation of the crowd into a sustained, high performance community.

Choose the CEO, prescribe a process, position him so that he positions the community and make sure that the community is on a path of continuous improvement—sustained high performance.

The CEO selects a custodian of maps: CTO, Facilities Manager and other additional positions as required.

Selection of vice-presidents (VPs) for marketing, HR, finance, learning and development and establish time lines.

Position them in the appropriate quadrant by consensus of the group.

The CEO fixes true north, describes his compass function.

The VP-marketing outlines the market potential, business development plan and personnel requirements/product/market mix, pricing, targets.

VP-HR translates the business plan and organises the human component.

VP-Finance, the controller of weights and measures—metrics.

VP-L&D: his/her business is that we learn continuously.

Other roles: Regulators/industry associations/venture capitalists and the external public.

In the mornings we recollected our dreams to check whether our unconscious was aligned with our conscious. The process went on for six days. We climbed peaks and got glimpses of the blue ocean space and at times fell down to the valleys like Humpty Dumpty, but managed to gather ourselves together and continue on the journey.

The game continues, but we are back in our respective places of work. Are we back to the same place? Certainly not; we have moved ahead towards true north, 61 of us—a learning community.

The journey/process is on.

New IITs, IIMs and the Toyota recall

I was at a b-school, anchoring a workshop on accelerated learning when reports appeared in the media that Toyota had recalled 688,314 vehicles produced in China though no injuries or accidents were linked to the recall. The recall amounts to more than a year's sale of vehicles.

Soon after, I had this dream: I am waiting in front of the b-school I graduated from in 1981. There is a huge crowd of alumni waiting to register.

The b-school has a great reputation and has discovered that there have been some major glitches in all their graduates. The graduates have been responsible for systemic failures of grave dimensions, affecting the very survival of the planet. The alumni, me included, are waiting to register for a remedial programme. Their licences to practice have been revoked. I wake up from the dream with the fear of losing my job to realise that I do not have a job to lose and that I don't need a licence to do what I do for a living. Thank god, it is only a dream.

We share our dreams and news in the morning. We will soon have more IITs and IIMs. We are wonderful when it comes to numbers. The Toyota quality issue pales in comparison when we look at what the top of the pyramid does to the bottom. It is part of our programming to think of the world in terms of pyramids or sometimes as flat, reflecting our own inner landscapes. We perceive ourselves to be standing at the apex of the pyramid, from where the rest of humanity is down there.

We don't just leave it at that.

More questions follow: What is Indian about the Indian Institutes of Management? Are they b-schools or m-schools? If they are catering only to business why are they called management institutes? Is business not capable of meeting its own demand for managerial talent? Why should the government indulge in this business where it has no competence to talk about? Why do we want more of them when they have failed in meeting our technology and management challenges? Do US seeds germinate and take root in the Indian soil? Can copies be better than the original? Which Indian academic in management, working in India has the highest recall rate? Why is it that we don't even have a single technology or management breakthrough of world-class scale and size in proportion to the scale and size of the country? Why are we so hung up on numbers and blissfully unaware of quality? We say quality, quantity and time go into setting of standards and that standards, though essential, can also breed conformity and compromise on outstanding achievements, when we don't have any standards of our own?

Is there a moral to the story? Accelerated learning and making people ask questions is a tightrope walk. One cannot indulge in it without taking a position on some of these issues.

On 25 August 2008, we were witness to a different kind of Olympic event. Around 300 young people, average age 25, were celebrating their outstanding achievements and performance at work in the Trinity hall of the Taj Residency, Bangalore where I heard the following statement:

"We are meeting here a day after the Olympics, an Olympics where China made its century and we got away with the 'holy trinity'. It is appropriate that we meet in the trinity hall and discuss our performance, be it in Olympics or in our work. We need to celebrate performance even if they are not grand victories and we need to celebrate such winnings in the context of the community that made it possible. I congratulate all of you and those who have shown such brilliant planning of the event that we could discuss these issues in the most appropriate context. I thank you for making it possible for me to be part of this celebration of community and performance. It is also the most appropriate time for us to discuss and envision, as a community of practice, the heights of performance that we would scale in the coming years."

The average age of billionaires is 61. The Facebook CEO Mark Zuckerberg is the youngest of the lot at 23. Two out of every three of the billionaires are self-made like the welfare mom J.K. Rowling who made it to the list at 42. So it is not always an inheritance of wealth that takes us to the heights, but the story of how we leverage the inheritance that nature and history have given us. Our own Anil Ambani was the one with the fastest rate of growth. More people from China and India are making it to the history books. The combined worth of around 1,100 billionaires is around $3 trillion.

Many of my millionaire classmates, who were many times smarter than me, are not around to talk about their performance. I am sure each one of us would have a dream other than making it to the list of billionaires. If all of us have only billionaire dreams, it would be better to start looking for another planet. This brings us to the issue of metrics and criteria by which we measure success, performance and achievements. Is wealth the only measure of success or should we have multiple criteria? While we celebrate performance, we also need to remind ourselves that personal success needs to be balanced with many other aspects. One very important aspect among them is improvement in community, which in the first place made these achievements possible, as this alone will guarantee sustained high performance (SHP).

Abhinav Bhindra, the lone gold medallist at the Beijing Olympics from >1 billion Indians has been drilling holes on paper for twelve+ years. He was seven when he proved himself to be a sharp shooter. From taking the position to be a shooter to reaching the summit of achievement spans a journey of 18 years, with many a set back and smaller wins in between. For Michel Phelps, focused effort started at 13 and the crowning event happened at 23. Mastering of the process takes ten years or even more. It is most often a lonely journey. What would be more interesting to watch will be how these people continue to perform and rewrite the story of human potential? Bubka continues to perform off the field. Mapping the human potential would require a closer study of the exceptions, not just in athletics, but from as many perspectives as possible at different levels, individuals, institutions, communities, globally and at the level of the species.

We will remember the events and forget the process. We have a built in bias towards our birthdays, floods, festivals and feasts.

How did China top the 2008 Olympics? India too has a comparably large population. China won by design, India won by default. It is ironic that the same is true of performance in other areas too. If India does not perform, the world will not, because one in every six is an Indian and one out of every three of the poor in the world is also an Indian. While individual performance may happen in isolation, performing as a community involves complexity of a much higher order. Some communities have a history of continual improvement while others do not fare as well.

India offers complexity of the highest order which makes it all the more interesting to students of performance/achievement. No other country has the same kind of complexity of colour, religion, language and dialects. For over two thousand years it has remained in a slumber, very often basking in the glory of a far too distant past.

Personal growth to performance as a single community is a continuum and at some stage in the process, critical mass and velocity is achieved for the collective transformation. A small minority takes position as individuals. They decide early in life as to their purpose of being here. The direction of their journey is clear to them and they hang on tenaciously. Once they achieve that, some of them redefine their goals for the next phase in the journey. Some others take a position much later, during the course of the journey. Many do not take a position at all. They leave it to the astrologer, fate, destiny or default. As a nation, India prefers the astrologer to the management consultant.

Global standards apply to the metrics of performance as in the Olympics though the same is realised within the local context. The gardener needs to know the soil. Gardening skills from Silicon Valley would need to be localised for better results in Bangalore. Unless it performs better than Silicon Valley, it does not get into the metrics. Once you get into the record books, there is the problem of continuing to outperform the competition. We have outlined the problem of SHP. The two b-schools I attended and the work that I was involved with kept me conscious of the Indian and the developmental complexity—that one cannot imitate and compete with the competition since a copy can never be better than the original. Each one of us is in a unique situation or context and each one has to find choose his/her road. That applies to community too, regardless of the scale, be it organisations or nations. Yet some universals hold good which could accelerate the process. The challenge of creating community necessitates taking a common position, a coming together based on a shared vision. How do you create such a vision? Do we have something, a non-controversial reference point, around which communities can emerge?

We have very sophisticated systems to navigate the planet and beyond. Navigating through life is a more complex process where each one of us is left with multiple tools. For some it may be the astrologer or their particular brand of belief system. The multiplicity of maps is one of the blocks to a common journey. I remember a starlit night, by the banks of a river. Looking at the sky my teacher asked me: "What is the meaning of all this?" I had no answer, but there was a wish at the time that some day I would find it out. It took 25 years to resolve the issue of making sense of the world, to make a map.

6 Ps to make sense of the world

Purpose

Positioning

Potential

Performance

Process

Pay attention, to improvements

We are born like bullets going out of the gun. Who fired the shot? You did not unless you are a mystic who can say that you chose your time, parents and the place of your birth. We have inherited a body and mind from our parents and the past; the product of a process as old and as young as the universe. How does one convert this inheritance, make it our own, own it? This is where the 6 Ps come in.

Can a 100-year-old regenerate his body? Prior to regenerating the body one should regenerate the spirit, the meaning. The spirit is about the purpose. Why are we here? Is it just because we were born, by default? Or is there a design? One should be able to recognise the design, the purpose. The Indian Government has a Department of Ayush for Indian systems of medicine; to my knowledge the only one of its kind in the world. We had a science of life, Ayurveda, an inheritance from our past. The department deals with the science of life! The purpose is to live, defeat death is the basic premise of Ayurveda. The philosophy is in stark contrast to the mainstream understanding of health and healing wherein to fall ill is the order, which is self-fulfilling. In Ayurveda, to fall ill is an exception. Once we have a purpose for which we are ready to die, take a position, we will not die unless the purpose is achieved. This is what it means to take a position. So have an impossible dream and take the position that this is the 'purpose of my being here' if we want to outperform the competition, live longer, defeat death, gain market share, whatever. What do we learn from people with exceptional longevity, centenarians? Why do they go on? Many of them are healthier than the 20+ some things I mostly work with. They seldom go to the doctor and still have that sparkle in their eyes.

When purpose is absent, the potential of the body is not challenged and unless we challenge, stretch, we do not create the conditions for the potential to be expressed—Phelps, Bubka, Isinbayeva, Bhindra—as individuals.

The next step is to challenge these limits as a community of practice and pay attention to the process, the improvements that happen and the metrics. Improvements follow from new learning. The self, individual or community is the learner, hence the First Discipline. The 6 Ps are in place. There are more Ps, perspectives and the more we have, the better we are in touch with reality, and our solutions are likely to be more effective.

True north

Animals align themselves to the magnetic poles of the earth. They have a built-in compass/GPS function, courtesy nature, to keep them aligned and tuned to nature. The human situation is more pathetic than that of the animal. We need to work on developing some of these skills, an obvious disadvantage in exchange for free will and choice. It took us a long time to develop the compass to navigate the world. Technology has become very sophisticated and our maps of the planet and immediate neighbourhoods are near perfect. We can cover much more in a day than previous generations, can even go for a deep dive into outer space and come back with pin point precision.

Though mobility has improved rapidly, the vast majority of us still do not move out of our places of birth. There is a different kind of a journey which all humans undertake, the one of personal and community growth and development. How well equipped are we for this journey which is many times more complex than a journey across space?

Let us run a reality check.

What is the first requirement for a journey across space? We should make certain of our current position. Ask any number of people, and you are not likely to get this answer.

Ask: Where are we now? What is our current position? What makes us humans uniquely different from the animals, as a class?

Ask yourself and arrive at the answer. Ask the same to another 100 people you come across. We play this game in our workshops. We seldom get the right answer even with groups of people known for their brilliance. Quiz them on anything else under the sun you would get an answer though. It takes much more time to get the group to agree that our uniqueness as a class, which makes us distinct from the animal, is our ability to IMPROVE ourselves, the environment and community around us. If we don't improve and improve continually, can we claim to be human, that we learn and evolve? If we do not, we would be sub-animal. The human is the most threatened of all species. S/he is a threat to him/her self, to the environment and other life forms. The World without us would be much better off. Animals do not kill within the same species without any reason, but we do. They don't have cancer wards, asylums and old age homes. If we are to learn about community it is much better that we look at them than at us. So what has gone wrong with us?

Is humanness/community improving or on the decline? Are we civilised? If the emperor says he is the emperor we have reason to disbelieve what we hear. The same holds true of claims of being civilised and developed. As a child I remember that most of the adults in my village used to carry a dagger with them, not to fight wild animals but to protect themselves from others. Hardly a week would pass without some news of a murder for some silly reason. Today they don't, but in some 'more civilised, developed parts' of the world nearly every other man owns a gun. Who is more civilised/developed?

Who performs and what are the criteria for measurement? The southern coastal state of Kerala in India, unlike many other parts of the country, has more or less the same quality of life as that of a developed country like Sweden, the major differentiator being it has a much lower per capita income. Should we measure development by eco illiteracy or eco literacy? Who leaves a bigger ecological footprint, the rich or the poor? Do we recognise performance? Farmers commit suicide in some parts of India. Fishermen of south India are probably the best of primary producers, but are even poorer than the farmers. Drinking water has become costlier than milk. Farmers and fishermen are poor not because they are not productive but because the markets and those on top of the pyramids respect and listen to those with muscle and not the unorganised. No wonder we have a crisis of food security in the making.

Are we better off than the animals in terms of community? Are we mature, adults? Hitler is not dead; he still lives in us. Listen carefully to the new age messiahs, gurus, change agents and leaders. Adults only need data, information and they can lead themselves. Compare the salary structure of CEOs in Japan and the US vs. that of the shop floor worker, which shows that we are willing to entrust our fate to the commander-in-chief, rest all our hopes on a small number of men and women. We have very little faith in the wisdom of the community. We still would like to have leaders and followers, rather than self-manage. The result is Hitlers in camouflage. So do we learn? If we do, there should have been improvements across multiple facets which ultimately will lead to oneness, better community, environment and the assurance of a secure future.

What is progress if in 2,500 years we could not go beyond Buddha and Christ and in over 5,000 years we could not improve on the wisdom of the

Upanishads? What have we understood about sex and sexuality if we have to translate the *Kama Sutra*, a treatise of similar antiquity on sex and sexuality, into many languages?

WANTED—A new language of improvement

'Change is the only constant.'

What about change-less-ness?

We have more change masters than masters of improvement. Change can be good or bad, superficial or substantial. Look at the semantics. If one observes the language one can see the positions which give rise to such views from which the language originates. From such positions, improvements cannot happen. To cross the semantic swamp we need a new language, a LANGUAGE of improvement and PERFORMANCE which we could call Inglish. Inglish is more than Indian English, which, thanks to the British, is spoken by more people than in Britain and the US combined. When one learns a language other than one's mother tongue, every word is very new whereas for the native speaker the very same words have lost their depths of meaning. Familiarity takes away the depth and might even breed contempt. Inglish is a requirement because we have used up the communication potential of most languages; most of it as advertising taglines to promote shadows and substitutes (Brand X makes you a complete man and brand Y makes the complete woman. Where are all the complete wo/e/men?).

So we communicate, yet do not enhance true community. Such communication is the noise, the major barrier to connect and build bridges. We need a common language to connect the world as a single community. We could make machines talk to each other across multiple platforms. The next step is to do the same with the human so that man and the machine are aligned. The GUI took the computer to the masses, transcending the barriers of language. The visual has more bandwidth than any other stimuli and the NOW generation views rather than reads. Inglish has to be a visual language.

This is just to trigger a continuing dialogue. This work is not meant to be full-fledged with self-contained arguments. These are some thoughts on why we need a compass/GPS to fix our position and direction for the journey; to show us the TRUE NORTH, one for each one of us, since we cannot use somebody else's.

Designer lives! Greening our selves

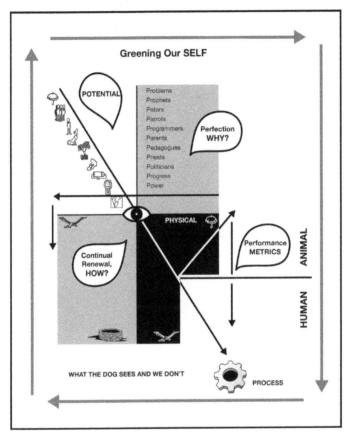

As I started writing this segment, I ran a search on Google with the term 'designer lives', but quickly abandoned it when I saw:

Designer lifestyle—26,400, 000 entries

Designer life coaching—14,400,000 entries

Designer sarees—869,000 entries

Designer sarees, pictures—2,280,000 entries

I also spent some time trying to find a coach with whom to air these ideas. I was not successful because I had modelled my theory on my understanding of two of my role models who could be life coaches. One was over 100 years old when he died (he ran out of work) and the other is 113 years old and still going strong.

So all that search amounted to nothing?

Not really, because now I know that Indians are slightly more interested in designer lifestyles than designer sarees and designer jewellery. The last time they were looking for somebody to head the national centre for design, they approached one of my neighbours who dabbles in jewellery design!

I turned my attention to *The Times of India* and an interview with Malcolm Gladwell. He says we are 'information rich and theory poor'. I do not agree. If dogs can 'see', what they 'see' will be worth a look.

My search had to be abandoned because most theories, in the long run, have not helped, even the proponents, other than getting some a flea span of attention.

Many gods die very young! At my age, I cannot afford to be taken for many more rides. I do, however, have several dialogue partners and we chat, often as we take a walk in the morning.

Why don't you stop theorising and get to the issue? Do you have a set of principles? Where do we begin?

Get ready for some mental jugglery.

We need to make a SHIFT.

We need to approach Potential, Performance, the WHY and HOW of the potential performance gap, simultaneously.

We need to take an informed position and be our SELF.

We need some simple metrics to be certain that we are on the PATH.

Well, that is juggling with too many balls at the same time.

It is now established that juggling improves your intelligence. The more the balls, the better it is. Most of us can manage just one or two at the same time.

Moreover, we have the four wheels, the engine (self) and the driver in place to begin the journey.

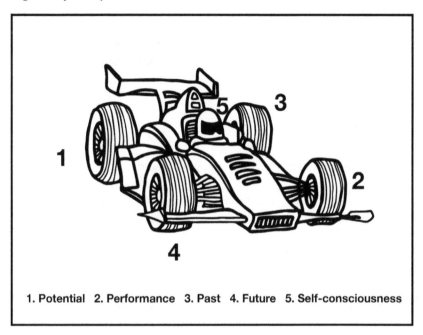

1. Potential 2. Performance 3. Past 4. Future 5. Self-consciousness

Wow. It is a DIY manual!

Yes, it is.

It is another day.

Which dog are you talking about? There are 162 dogs, the slum dog type, in our gated community and another 36 luckier (?) ones owned by dog lovers who have taken permission from the managing committee of the community headed by an animal rights activist. The dialogue happens after my morning walk. There is this one dog which seeks us out and joins us on a regular basis.

Of the 162 dogs why is it that this one finds it worthwhile to join us?

It knows that you are a recruitment manager who knows the difference between dog-ness and human-ness! It sniffs out the difference between the rest of us and the one who knows what it is to be human!

Wow. That's an idea. Dogs could be used in recruitment. It would be more effective than most of our metrics. Perhaps I could patent the idea and leave my job to the dogs!

Well it is coming to that very soon. There are agencies that teach us to mimic animals or the rest of nature as if they hold the key to human-ness.

Why mimic?

Imitation is the sincerest form of flattery.

It is such a headache to think, know and understand.

But mimicry is a kind of pathetic humour that comes out of help-less-ness. When we don't have the original we make do with copies.

When we hear the next guru talking of inner ecology, take it that the inner desertification (or interior decoration?) is complete!

What does this dog, the other dogs and the pet dogs see?

Well dogs, as a community, seem to believe in the steady state theory since at the last count too we had around 160 dogs. They know what dog-ness is all about. With every one out of three of us likely to get cancer, one in ten to get a heart attack and with all the other odds taken together, it shows that dogs are healthier than humans. We live a dog's life!

Somebody I knew was chased by a pack of dogs on a beach. He had no option but to get into the water. The dogs stood howling on the shore and were chased away by the life guards. He lived for another six months and took the exit route on his own. The dogs knew, it seems.

Well what does this 'special dog' in the visual see?

This dog sees the two paths. It sees that most of what we see as progress is a fall, and together we are heading in the wrong direction. It also sees the path that we should take, the path of human-ness, continuous improvement, real progress.

It would probably not join us if we start imitating the other 161 dogs!

This dog knows. Most facts are stranger than fiction.

The Pipers of Hamlin, Wall Street

We are back at it again with the special dog for company.

The master said, 'be the child'. Where on earth are the children? They have vanished with the Pipers from Wall Street!

The children are so 'well informed' these days that I feel I am an ignoramus. They know what is in and what is out and I am certainly out by those standards.

How do I take an 'informed position' and be my SELF? How can I be my SELF when there is such a well-intentioned, charity-driven, messianic attack on our collective SELF, the most threatened and endangered entity in our current context.

I am not complete in my SELF without a fan following (my Twitter count of followers is zilch) or following somebody in sincere flattery.

Is there a gold standard certification in these things? I see that every guru of the day, self-certifies his/her claims! Most of them are younger than me, have never been married, have never raised any children.

Another set of pipers?

I am afraid I would prefer not to follow anybody and drive away potential disciples who would rob me of my silence.

Well in that case you cannot be a GURU.

How long will gold be the standard? When everything else is of no value, can gold have any value? If everybody does a Gandhi or Thoreau what happens to the economy?

You haven't contributed much to the economy. You are taking more than what you give to it. You have not been ill for a long long time, which means you are contributing to the recession. You don't use any cosmetics. How will the economy recover?

Are we getting to the age of The Descent of Money?

The 'piped music' is so enchanting that I don't want to unplug and listen to my SELF which is under attack from all the four directions, from the bottom and the top—24x7x720. Perhaps what we consider music is noise which has silenced the silence, the real music, from a dog's perspective.

We wonder where all the children have disappeared. They have lost their innocence and with it the wise men too have vanished. The pipers have been doing a very good job.

Look at all the exercise freaks. They are all plugged in, connected, wired to their iPods, iPhones, iTouch, iBook, iSpouses. It is a connected world! There is very little else to be connected and taken over by the machines. Sci-fi has become the reality.

In spite of all the stretching, many of my one time friends vanished in their 40s.

The problem can be abstracted as: i >I or self >SELF

We cannot solve the puzzle without a decision compass that would help us find the directions and fix our position. The four directions are the four P balls that we juggle around—Potential, Performance/metrics, Perfection and Psychodynamics. (Continual renewal/ Continual Learning/Continuous Improvement, Kaizen, whatever you choose to call this wheel of the car/the learning engine)

What is a learning engine?

A learning engine improves on its previous best performance. It feeds itself on waste, a fusion engine. There is no cost for learning. The ROI is always positive, never a recession.

I hope you will stop with the four balls!

I was about to pull out more smaller balls from each of the four big balls.

That is enough for the day, time for a break.

(B . . . s to you. I could almost hear it)

The next day:

What is the gap between self and SELF?

This is the space between the two paths, what we call the blue ocean space, the solution space or the problem space depending on which position one takes. This represents the unrealised potential, the gap between the best of individual realisation of potential and the best of the collective potential of the human.

KISS!

Example: PCD lived for >100 years while the life expectancy for males in this context was 72 the normality of the time. The potential/performance gap is 28 years if we take just this one dimension. To make it simple we don't take into account the quality of life of the masses against the quality of life that PCD enjoyed or any of his other achievements.

If we consider the case of SRC, 113+, who is still working and hopes to work for more years we get an idea of what potential is and where the masses are! We cannot really fix an upper limit to potential, but we can chart out the broad contours of the direction of the path.

I get a rough idea of the direction that we are talking about.

As we move forward we will be able to see what is beyond the next bend in the road.

The visual also suggests that a good part of our behaviour is sub-animal!

This is our shadow side, the porn that greases the web engine, the medicines, drugs, cosmetics, the years wasted in asylums, prisons, lives lost in conflicts, suicides, terrorism, so on and so forth. Unrealised potential is the root cause of all our problems.

When we say 'be myself', what we mean is be my true SELF as distinct from what we have come to believe as dictated by the noise around us.

WHY this gap exists and HOW to bridge or narrow it are the other two balls.

It is in relation to these four directions that one can fix the position just as a compass or GPS would deliver what they are designed to.

There are two kinds of positions as in the case of the lighthouse and the sailing vessel, the invariant and the variant. The ship has to change course in relation to the lighthouse.

Be more specific.

As a surgeon, I take the position that I am a professional, which means I have a set of competencies that I practise in a specific domain, which I continue to perfect over a life time. I am also bound by a code of behaviour that expects me to hold my client's well being as my overriding principle, which provides the context in which my performance becomes measurable. The standards are the most challenging. In case of non-delivery, the surgeon will not be able to go scot free as the Pipers of Hamlin, Wall Street.

I hope you see the invariant position and the variant positions in the journey of the professional. The invariant is: come what may, even at the cost of my life, I will remain a professional. It is a do or die position. The variant is: as I move ahead on the journey I continue to improve my competencies and scale higher and higher levels of perfection.

It is time we pull out the balls within the balls. The journey from our animal self (i) to the human (I) begins here.

You are a pain. Enough for the day.

I believe in the 'PIA theory of motivation'.

Good day, JM.

My Inglish style sheet says, "Break the container, get the content."

What Sanskrit is to Prakrit, Inglish is to English.

Hope you too see what the dog sees or 'god' sees—the big picture. The headwind is strong. It is better for a take-off than sailing.

Another morning, another conversation

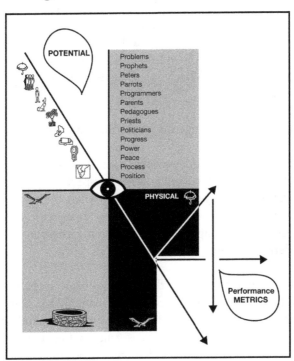

The dog is in attendance and we continue.

"The world is chaotic, disorganised and vexing. Medicine is no exception," says one of my dialogue partners and friends, the surgeon. He advises governments on health policy issues in addition to his hectic and often punishing routine. The only issue on which we come together is our morning routine; on all the rest we take positions that are poles apart.

This is why inner ecology is important. If we don't find order in our own self, what we see in the world outside is chaos, disorder and when you advise the world, you could be contributing to more of the chaos and disorder. The intentions are always good but the effect is disastrous.

Since you come at the end of the assembly line in the health system where surgery is the only option, most of what you see influences your world view.

That is ridiculous.

The more you see the conflicts, violence, absence of harmony outside, you are more likely to be caught up in it. You become what you pay attention to and come to believe that this is the nature of reality. The opposite also is true—the more you look for order and organisation, one becomes more ordered in one's own SELF. You will then be contributing more to order than chaos. The choice is yours. What you see depends on where you stand, your position.

What are you driving at? Change my career/position at this stage?

I am not suggesting anything. I say that this should not be your invariant position, which would emerge from a larger perspective of the true potential; a better understanding of the design, so that when the system goes out of order, one can restore order without resorting to extreme measures. These extreme measures are contingent on taking such a position and are nothing but belated inferior solutions.

When our car or the tablet breaks down we go back to the design to put it right. Our system doesn't come with a user manual that helps us diagnose and bring the system back to order. Without understanding the design we cannot decide whether the system is true to the design. Most of our expectations are based on ill-informed assumptions about the design and we pay a heavy price for it.

To repeat, our most well-meaning intentions create the most disastrous results.

You are getting ready for more jugglery.

Simplicity is a noble goal, but it should not be at the cost of truth. What I suggest is that we go up together and get the lunar perspective. Perhaps we might come to share the dog's perspective.

Shoot.

We will first take a look at the potential quadrant, the front, left wheel of the learning engine. Though when we drive the four wheels move together, the car is now at rest and we are looking at each of the wheel assemblies in isolation. In juggling, all the balls should be in the air but we are just studying the ball which is at rest. The eye at ground zero stands for the compass perspective. The compass is hidden here. To use the compass one has to

When we set right the alignment, all the four wheels need to be corrected at the same time because any small change in any one affects all. To do that we need to understand the design of the other two wheels also.

What about the metrics?

The process involved in metrics comes first. It is about reflecting on performance with the design in mind and understanding that the system is designed to continually improve on its previous best performance in terms of quantity, quality and time. All metrics are approximations and it is not an exact science. The actual indicators, criteria of performance, could be quite simple which shows us the progress to true north and reduction in WASTE. We will come back to the issue of metrics after an overview of all the sub-assemblies.

It is becoming dense. Let us take a break.

You claim to be a virtual permaculturist?

My father was the original. He believed that doing nothing is Doing Everything. It took me a lifetime to understand what he stood for. By the time, all the land was gone and I could only be a virtual perma-'culturist'!

Permaculture is about understanding the design of nature and allowing the design to express itself; not to stand in the way of nature. The templates of nature are perfect and beyond improvement. Our best efforts to improve them most often fail. We need to live with them.

Learning has no cost. It always fetches the best ROI. The metrics need to take into account the future savings of costs associated with not learning (For example savings from avoiding a cardiac arrest).

We need to start with culture before we get into permaculture.

What is common to the Amazon forest dweller and the Wall Street investment banker is the basic template. One stakes his claim to be civilised and from the first world while the other does not make any such claims. One is blissfully unaware of the design whereas the other claims to have all the keys to unlock potential. We need to strike the middle path between the two.

When Vasco Da Gama reached the Malabar coast, he was shocked to find the women going topless. Now when the tourists come to the very same beaches and bare themselves, they are ogled at. The wheel has come a full circle in just around five centuries! It is not even two centuries since we abolished slave labour. We abolished it when we found better ways to achieve the very same purpose 'in style'. The same goes for dictatorships.

Why does the emperor shout that he is the emperor?

The emperor is not certain that he is the real one!

You have a Freudian fixation with the Ps.

My professor NSR was much better at it. He would juggle with 100s of Ps and make them dance in the air, while my professor of marketing was juggling with just 4 Ps. I am told that he has gone up to 7 now. I am just using around 40 Ps; the very minimum to show you what I want you to see. This is a minor fixation, synchronicity at work.

Why do you always take recourse to myths?

Beware of myths because they will survive all the mass wipeouts. It is better to understand them so that we go beyond them. The myth is the key to our unconscious, the silent sub-surface driver of the engine, a source of mis-alignment. We will get to this much later.

Where do we go on from here?

We take a look at the other two wheels, the engine and the driver of the learning engine.

It is getting complex.

Complexity is the best challenge to stretch you. It is a headache, but I peddle a 'one minute cure' for headaches.

Complexity feeds me.

Perfection and Psychodynamics

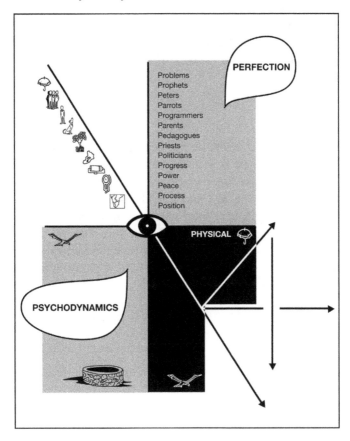

The dialogue continues:

After Christmas and the New Year we wait for the next feast /festival, Easter?

We need to celebrate them on the same day, reinventing time. Every moment, day, is a birth, death and resurrection. Celebrating the new decade makes better sense. We would like to wish you a new decade of real progress and sustained continuous improvement. Given the pace at which we improve, a decade makes a better time horizon to put all the improvements and disappointments in perspective. When we make the shift to REAL from linear time, time does not run out; it stretches out.

You have always been a champion of laziness and you have invented another jugglery to substantiate it. So wish you a still slower decade to laze around.

Hope you cross the decade setting a new record of doing NOthing and continue to haunt us.

I am not lazy. I work very hard to remain a contrarian. I work very hard to improve my Jowar count and am very pleased with my progress, improvements.

Jowar?

It is a specially designed exercise for seniors, a combination of jogging, walking and running. I hope to join the veterans' Olympics post 2020. I also work very hard not to make any money, not to leave any footprints including the carbon one, to consume less and stretch myself at the physical, mental and spiritual planes. I fight very hard not to go in for a new car. I give more than what I take, live more with less and make sure that my output is always more than the inputs. I work on the fusion mode. I had to work very hard to make that shift from the fission mode. There is always a tendency to slip back and I have always to be on guard.

Let us continue from where we digressed. It is time to look at the other two wheels, quadrants.

You always talk in pairs, at least two balls at a time.

That is true of everything. A photon is a particle and wave. Black makes no sense without white. So here is the counter pair to Potential and Performance. We have Perfection and Psychodynamics to juggle with.

Psychodynamics, why the jargon after using the language of the shop floor so far?

Just to impress you!

We started with the assumption that if it takes an Einstein to understand reality, we don't want any part of that. We have been accused of being too thin, un-academic, unsubtle and so on. Google it, if you want a definition. We don't attempt definitions and we don't have any institutional memory other than our personal ones. I have freed my memory banks of all data available by a simple search so that there is no clutter within. In the post-Google age, forty hours or even less of learning is all it takes to pick up the essentials to be really successful in life. We have been testing the hypothesis for two decades now.

How do you define success?

We don't know.

I wish I hear this more often.

Each one will have to do that according to his/her standards. For us, if you haven't got into accidents of any kind, on the road or off the road (relationships), not been ill but improving in heath, making as much money as you have decided to make and your family and friends are also doing equally well, we would say that one is successful.

What about perfection?

Perfection is embedded in us but we don't want to accept it. Most businesses would go out of business if we accept it including the business of education. Guardians of knowledge, custodians of the keys, the gatekeepers would not relish it. Take a look at the list of gatekeepers (the four classes of programmers) in the top right quadrant of the FD framework.

You would be thrown out at the gates itself!

There is this alignment problem between the two wheels of the learning engine. Paying attention to this will be worth the effort. This defines the learning requirements for the journey. Once we recognise the issue, the system, over time, will move towards a dynamic steady state. It is good to be confused because ultimately there will be a resolution. We will not have butter without churning the cream. It is said 'ask and ye shall be given'.

Make it clearer. I have a low tolerance for ambiguity.

There is the ideal and our understanding of the ideal; perfection and our understanding of perfection. It is like God created us in his image and we recreate him in our image. Our image is that of the God who art in heaven, a master-slave relationship which forms the master template for all our relationships. No dialogue is possible from these positions. The adult will never be born.

Should we bring God in here?

If for most people God stands for the ideal, perfection, quality, love, order, life, negentropy, why not bring in God? I am yet to come across a non-believer. The atheist too is a believer since he believes that there is no God. I am yet to find an Indian who does not believe in his astrologer! For him his astrologer is God. The astrologer works on the premise that there is order and predictability not only in the case of clockwork systems, but similar order and predictability exists in the case of higher level systems too and in the very long run perfection will prevail.

In the short run all of us will be dead!

If God stands for life and we stand for death, this pair certainly needs our attention.

More juggling?

Not yet. We are getting ready for the real juggling.

What do you mean by lighthouses?

Isaac Newton (1642-1727) continues to be our lighthouse since we are, collectively, yet to move from the clockwork paradigm. Einstein (1879-1955) ought to have stood on Darwin's (1809-1882) shoulders.

But the lighthouse industry is extinct. R. L. Stevenson (1850-1894) foresaw the demise of the industry and left his tradition in time. His fiction was brought under the lens by Carl Jung (1875-1961). The artist always SEEs ahead of the scientist.

We don't need lighthouses anymore. The new technologies mimic the meta framework of nature much better. The second coming is that of the common Buddha, who will SEE directly without intermediation by the gatekeepers. Visual literacy, not language, helps us SEE together as a community.

So the basic divide is between clocks and living systems, chaos and order, life and death, default and design?

The map shows that there is no divide, but we still believe that there is a divide or unity still remains beyond our collective experience. Reality is what we believe to be true. We are co-creators of death, not life. We see inheritance in place of emergence because of the positions we take. To co-create life we need to shift our positions for good.

There are more Ps to be explained.

Problems: From our position, they are opportunities; the more complex they are, the more challenging. It is fun.

Prophets: Take the vision, bury the dead.

Peters: The guardians of lighthouses sans the vision of the prophets drive us away from climbing up the lighthouses to take a peek. That too is in the fitness of things.

Programmers: We come preloaded with a program to fail. The winner stakes all, which includes all the past programming.

Parrots: A copy can never be better than the original, but copies do come in handy. Why reinvent the wheel?

Power: There is power which makes one free and also power that leads to the making of slaves. The path to spirituality is through the thick forest of sex. Most get lost here. Narcissus to Pygmalion and Galatea set the direction of the path and we are yet to go beyond Narcissus. Sex drives the economy and the markets. Sex and power come packaged in the same container.

What about the bird and the semi dark circle in the bottom left quadrant?

This is what happens when we learn. There is a bolt of lightning that connects the small with the big, local with the global, micro with the macro, like the proverbial apple that fell on Newton, sparking the connect of that very local event with the grand design of the physical world.

What about Jung's *The Red Book*?

The book is a pointer to the solution, not the solution itself.

Why so?

All the reason, logic and analysis that have given us technology, will not help us if we are primarily driven by the unconscious. The unconscious will drag us down and we will never achieve take off velocity. Myths, fantasy, fiction and hyper reality will rule us rather than reality. Artificial intelligence will continue to be more fashionable than intelligence and intuition. Magicians and pipers will continue to fool us with substitutes in place of real magic and real miracles. We need to bring back magic and miracles to our daily routine.

Real magic and miracles!

A miracle is something that cannot be explained by the known laws of nature. When we admit that there will always be unknowables but they are not our enemies, the complete system will be working with us. When the whole of nature is working for us, the true potential is unlocked. There is nothing hiding in the dark to pounce on us. This is freedom from the unknown. The drag is killed. There is nothing super-natural when we understand the nature of nature. We need better keys to align with the unknown and that is how we got into designing dreams.

Can we really design dreams?

Yes, if we can get rid of all the accumulated garbage. Look to Shaili, one of our tribe. She has been doing it for the last few years. She had very little garbage to get rid of.

When we align our SELVES/SELF with the unconscious, we have the best ally and we are no more driven by the unknown which is a huge step to mastery of the self. We are not driven, but we are in the hot seat; in charge of driving the learning engine. We become the magicians, moving to centre stage from being spectators. We are responsible to ourselves and the journey is about continual learning and improvement. We are here to learn.

There are two more Ps.

Peace: If we find it within, we will find it outside us too.

Process: Nature is in process. We too are. Let the process go on . . . There are no full stops, a destination; the journey continues. The direction is fixed, the true north.

Go with the process?

Which process are you talking about, the process of inheritance or emergence?

We need to see both together and the outcome, net improvements, the progress (one more P) towards true north.

It is much more complex than a Rubik's cube.

It is. But, there is a solution and always a still better one. And then the perfect one. We are on the path to perfection. We may never reach the perfect solution.

Are we through with the wheels? What about the engine and the driver?

We are through with the rough design. We will need to get into the detailed design of the engine and the driver. That is for another time.

We have covered the generics, not the specifics which are personal and situational. It takes some time to become comfortable with the rough design.

PS: To our Wordsmith. If the word is your sword, what is your battle?

Between the Haiti earthquake and the day of the max eclipse, it is a journey of over 1,000 years to the next one of a similar kind.

See you there.

Community intelligence

Are we intelligent as a species?

Yes and no.

We are not intelligent going by many aspects of our performance. We are much more 'endangered' than any other species. We are a threat to our SELVES and the other flora and fauna. We are more ill than the animals, we kill within the species without any reason which no other species does and we are the only threat to life. So we need an UNPROJECT—the new Noah's ark—to protect and conserve the species.

But how will you identify a pair? What will be the criteria for selection? If we pull it off, the species and the environment will be very safe.

We have been asking large groups of some very 'intelligent people', what is the unique differentiator between the human and the rest of the species. We never got the answer right the first time without some triggering and a process of creating agreement. Unless we agree, we cannot achieve community.

If we are not intelligent as a species, how can there be intelligent people around?

We now understand intelligence so 'much better'—with different versions of it. We claim that intelligence can be taught. Another business is in the making. Which parent wouldn't want it? Of all the 'intelligences' my personal favourites are the gender and community versions. Why are we not intelligent? One reason is the way we understand intelligence, without seeing and relating the connection with the One and the Many, the whole and the parts, intelligence and Intelligences, the different or 'differentiated versions' and the undifferentiated. We need to integrate and differentiate simultaneously. We are intelligent, if we go by our potential to be intelligent, by design but not intelligent going by our history and performance.

The emperor has no clothes but claims very loudly that he is The Emperor. What we think of as great progress, an ascent and evolutionary progress is but a descent, the great fall.

So what makes us human?

The community learning engine

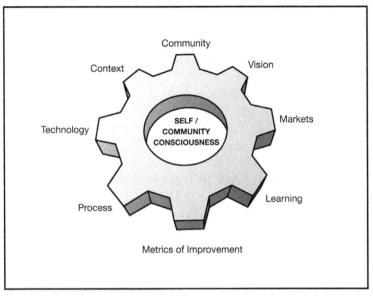

Technology and markets are levers to bring about improvement. Some communities have achieved remarkable progress using them. But conventional measures of improvement fail to grasp the cost at which such improvements are achieved. Economic growth needs to be balanced with improvement in community. Some communities have achieved a better physical quality of life at a much lower cost to community and there are also communities like the ecosystem people where in spite of improvements in growth, corresponding improvements in quality of life have not materialised. The focus here is on how a particular community responds to the challenges of managing technology and markets along with improvements in community. One way to assess the quality of community is to monitor the number of suicides, crimes, addictions of various types, mental illness and similar indicators.

The learning engine is capable of continually improving on its past performance against all odds. The focus of metrics needs to be on improvement of community as reflected in reduction in waste—conflicts, violence, illness, suicides, crime, infant mortality and in realising unrealised potential such as quality of life and environment, longer lifespans and improvement in wellness.

It is the core which drives the process of improvement that reflects on its position, direction and corrects itself to ensure that the process is in tune.

143

Context—global or local, but glocal-ness is recognised.

Technology and markets need to be used as levers to enhance community.

Vision—renewed continually and aligned for sustained high performance.

Development is the most complex process that needs catalysts. The catalysts do not burn out in the process, but in their absence the process is not initiated and sustained.

Storytelling—Walking out of our shadows

Pygmalion coaxes Galatea out of stone and she comes alive. The Pygmalion position is that of the facilitator who catalyses performance, who has audacious expectations of performance, of sustained high performance, moving from peaks to still higher peaks. The expectation is not unfounded because Pygmalion has experienced the magic of sustained high performance. Every stone may not be good enough to be turned into a beautiful statue, but every human has the potential to be an outstanding performer.

How does Galatea respond to the hard knocks by Pygmalion in his efforts to coax her out of stone? If she can see the results of the hard knocks, she would certainly enjoy the process because she can see that between the caterpillar and the butterfly, the seed and the tree, there is a world of a difference. She knows that this is the moment of truth that she had been waiting for ages. Like what happens in the story of Ahalya and Rama.; Ahalya has been waiting for that divine moment of Rama's coming. The process is certainly complex and miraculous and the catalyst is integral to sustained high performance. Pygmalion and Rama play the role of catalysts, facilitators, in the transformational process.

People are waiting like Ahalya. Nations are waiting. Billions are waiting, like the farmers and fishermen, at the 'bottom of the pyramid' essentially because the top is unable to connect with the bottom in the exchange and valuation process. It is debatable who is at the bottom and who is at the top. If you change the criteria of measurement, the bottom will become the top and vice versa. For example who leaves a larger ecological footprint? The cathedrals remain to be built.

Bubka, Isinbayeva and others do it over and over. They take the position—I can and I will do it. I will outperform myself, again and again. Can we take the same position, as individuals, a team and as a community? Nations have taken such positions. Kishore Mahbubani asks this question to all Asian countries—*Can Asians Think?*—like Singapore has been thinking together since 1965.

As individuals we don't have to go on waiting for miracles to happen or for another prophet to turn up. While billions are waiting, we can have islands of sustained high performance around each one of us. The islands will eventually connect together for that defining era of collective transformation. We are in that transition phase of achieving critical mass and gaining take off velocity of the process, of more and more of us transforming our SELVES to catalysts for the tectonic shifts.

So what is your position? Pygmalion and Galatea got to come together on this; the alchemist's marriage. Later, Galatea will take the Pygmalion position and the process continues.

Back to Bubka and Isinbayeva: what is the pole that we are talking about, the lever? How long is the lever? Where is the fulcrum? How does a community of practitioners ALIGN and LEVERAGE themselves for sustained high performance. The longer the lever, the greater the mechanical advantage.

Metrics—The Community Consciousness Quotient

Less is more. At 64, I am not a gadget geek. Yet I love my mobile and the way it has been shrinking over the few years that I have been using it, accommodating more and more of my requirements. I have accumulated a lot of electronic waste over the years like my compass, VCP, music players of progressively smaller sizes and better quality, the desktops. Very soon my notebook too will join the list. We are consuming less of the material and deriving much more. Small is beautiful and smaller is still better. The tangible is shrinking and the intangibles are scaling up, becoming more tangible than the tangibles. Capital too has been shrinking, being substituted by intellectual capital, brawn by brains. My wants (not needs) too have shrunk, at least most of those that I considered important in my 30s and 40s, like a gas-guzzling SUV. Being glued to my LCD screen and not travelling to work I have earned a few carbon credits, not using my car except for the weekend shopping trip. (It would be much better to dispose it off and hire one when I really need it). But all needs do not vanish with age, perhaps they grow with age. The need for community (to be connected), quality and richer experiences, the need to learn and express myself. Sometimes more is less. Intelligence has evolved into intelligences, multiple intelligences, emotional, gender, social and, in the process, we have become less intelligent in community consciousness. So the metrics need to take into account improvement in community within and without along with conventional measures of improvement in performance.

Community Consciousness Quotient (CCQ) is an imperative for Sustained High Performance. The absence is killing us in many ways, which we don't need to go into.

Aligning with the unknown

Connect to your best friend.

Why should I?

How do I diagnose whether the unknown is working for or against me?

How do I align myself with the unconscious, the unknown and the unknowable?

What are the payoffs of aligning with the unknown?

If this makes sense, go to the next:

Start here:

Build the lighthouse

Light the beacon, Watch out

Notes from lighthouse keepers: Feather Girl and Dream Catcher (more in Chapter 6)

Before: Self, by default

After: SELF, By design

CHAPTER 5

Metaphoria of Transformation

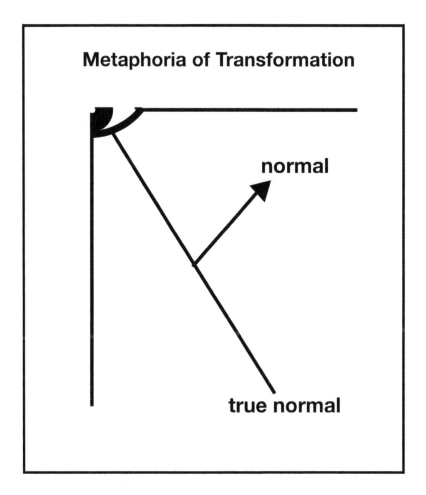

Are we aware of this 'other' stranger in us?

The image points to the gap between the perceived normal and the true normal. This is the direction of the transformational journey and this deep urge is at the root of our consumption, real or substitutes.

Successful brands connect to this deep urge in a very powerful way.

Every guru, astrologer and consultant knows this. When we are unaware of this stranger in us we are likely to be driven by him.

Promises and Placebos fill this vacuum. Powerful brands are perceived as vehicles of transformation. Myths, Metaphor and stories connect to this vacuum. Stories sync brains.

Solutions emerge once the image is formed

The following threads to stories and metaphor can be used in many ways. It is for the facilitator to customise them for the group and the context. They are hooks to connect to the internal and external territories to unearth something that people already know at deeper levels.

The differently abled child and the teacher

There's this child who is unable to pick up maths. For him, everything is one. He's shown the door by the teacher. Many years later, the teacher meets him on the road. The youth reminds him of the child once thrown out of school by the teacher. The old man is curious. "How do you write one now," he asks. The young man points to a rock on the horizon and draws a line in the air. The rock splits into two and moves apart.

The facilitator works with the group to connect to the rationale of the story.

Mental maps—the eagle's gift

We've seen the story of the eagle and the frogs in the well in Chapter 1. To jog our memory, here it is again—A community of frogs live in a deep well. Alongside the well is a tall tree on which an eagle nests.

The frogs have always lived in the deep well from which they have never gone out, nor can they move out of it on their own; they only dream of the external world. Every night the granny frog tells bedtime stories to the young ones in the well. Most of the stories have been passed down over generations with an occasional improvisation here and there. Often, the eagle listens to the stories.

One morning, when the thermals had begun rising in the air, the eagle swoops down into the well, grasps one little frog in its claws and rises up with the thermals. The heights and the fear of death grip the little one. The eagle stays with the thermal, circling the well and when it finds that the little one has calmed down a bit, it releases the frog from its claws. The frog lands back in the same well, unhurt, still afraid and probably elated. During the free ride the frog had opened its eyes for a brief moment to get a glimpse of the world outside the well. The eagle returns to the tree waiting for the sun to set, to hear the new stories.

Each participant in the group writes a story. The facilitator gives feedback based on participants' stories. Switch the role of facilitators so that the facilitators don't come to assume that they are the eagles. One has to be an eagle at times and a frog at others, depending on the context.

The human condition is like that of the frog in the well. Our mental maps are influenced by the 'well' we live in. They are improved with every bit of learning. The developmental process involves revision and improvement of the mental models to maps.

The Chandrasekhar effect

Chandrasekhar is a very saintly soul with a weakness for alcohol. One morning we found him in front of his regular hangout. Chandrasekhar was relieved to meet a familiar face. Though drunk he did not want to be humiliated. "Where am I," he asked.

We take the most fundamental for granted, which takes us further away from reality. When our basic assumptions about our current position are wrong, we will not reach home. Any process of improvement calls for fixing a starting position, deciding on the direction and reflecting/reviewing with reference to the starting position.

A large number of people were asked this question as to what our basic needs are and the first reply is always the textbook answer, "food, shelter, and clothing." For someone for whom life is meaningless, these things do not matter.

When people are asked how many sides the coin has, the answer is always the same—two; though with a little bit of clarification they will soon shift their original positions.

The Taj Mahal

Emperor Shajahan asked three stonecutters who were working on the construction of the Taj Mahal the same question: "What are you doing."

The three answers were:

"I am earning a living."

"I am polishing stones, and I am the best stonecutter available."

"I am building a monument which is an expression of the love of the emperor for his beloved. And this stone that I am polishing will be the corner stone of the monument."

It is obvious that the third stonecutter is more likely to meet the standards for quality and quantity. It is also evident that if all three are to meet these and other standards—of effectiveness, excellence and zero defects—the third stonecutter's vision has to be shared. When we work more and more with intangibles and the slave driver is replaced by one's own self, it becomes all the more difficult but essential to keep the network as one, connected. This story is an Indian adaptation of the tale of the stonecutters building a Cathedral.

Indra and the pigs—Resistance to change

Indra, the Hindu god of rain and thunderstorms and the lord of heaven, once transformed himself into a pig to experience why pigs enjoy wallowing in the mud. Now, he doesn't want to leave his comfort zone, until Narada, the impish divine sage, finds him in the mud and with great effort brings him back to his former self. It is quite 'normal' that we get stuck with poor performance and come to accept this as the limit of our possibilities; till a compelling experience/crisis or vision might lift us out of the situation.

Frog soup

This story is quoted in two popular books on management, *The Renewal Factor* (Robert H. Waterman) and *The Fifth Discipline* (Peter M. Senge). The frog in water that is cold initially enjoys the increasing warmth of the water in which it is immersed and by the time the heat is unbearable, the frog is immobilised and incapable of escaping from death. The process of continual renewal is the opposite of this, whereby individuals, institutions or a community continually respond to the environment and improve their contexts. The process is qualitatively different and most often ignored in the preoccupation with the short term. It is more the norm than the exception that companies lose half their employees every four years, half their customers in five, and half their investors in less than twelve months. The returns on investment, yield rate of stocks, market capitalisation or increase in the value of ESOPs by themselves are not sufficient measures of success. Besides shareholders and targeted market segments, corporates need to be concerned about the internal and, the broader, external community too.

The gun shot/ The two roads

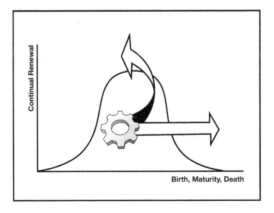

The road by design and by default, and the moment of truth.

What we believe as mature, normal, is a HABIT, history, the roadblock.

The system at physical birth is comparable to the bullet that leaves the barrel of a gun. The bullet is helpless to influence its trajectory.

Most systems, individuals or institutions seldom go beyond this level without that choice; a conscious decision to evolve, becoming aware of the position, direction and reflecting on progress. When it happens, the bullet goes into orbit.

The linear is the road by default; the road to death, accidents, burnout and the road on which time runs out.

The other is the road to eternity, continual renewal and timelessness by CHOICE; the conscious decision to be on the road to continual IMPROVEMENTs, creating the future NOW, by DESIGN—a future that is better than the present.

The gun shot does not have the potential to become aware of the self. Individuals and organisations do. They are capable of self-observation and self regulation, which implies the possibility of improvement. This is what qualifies us to be termed human. The cannon shot that goes out of the cannon has no possibility of becoming aware of itself and the outcome is already determined at the moment of its departure from the cannon. But the more advanced of human creations, like those of sophisticated machines, do have more and more of self regulation built into them.

Thus in the case of space vehicles and satellites, the extent of self regulation and the possibility of controlling the behaviour of the system from outside the system increases. The extent of self regulation, the possibility of reflecting on one's behaviour, and even laughing at it, is what draws us apart as a class. In the case of the cannon shot, gravity operates mercilessly and ultimately the shot is overtaken by it when it reaches terra firma. In the case of individuals and organisations, it is the vision that keeps them going. The vision is liable to be corrupted and needs to be renewed continuously. Just as gravity operates continuously, the forces of decay too is natural to all systems. In nature decay and renewal are continuous and it follows that for organisations to sustain growth, the effort at renewal too needs to be continuous.

Ashram and the prophets

There is an ashram that is in dire straits, with four sanyasins struggling to make ends meet. There was a time when crowds flocked to the ashram. One of the sanyasins has a bright idea to seek help from another sanyasin in a distant place. The 'consultant' sanyasin sends them back with just one piece of advice: 'One of you is a prophet'. The four are unable to agree on which one of them is the prophet, but over time the ashram renews itself and recovers its lost glory. This story is about the quality and process of leadership, creating and renewing vision and shared values.

Complex vs. simple—Tools and redundancy

$2 \times 2 = 4$

$4 \times 4 = 16$

$16 \times 16 = 256$

$256 \times 256 = ?$

Time

T ranscendental

I llusion

M ystic entanglement

E ternity

Mastery of time involves going beyond the ordinary or common to the transcendental experience of time. The common understanding is very essential to deal with the day to day world, but this is never the complete story. It is only a partial truth (illusion). Time/timelessness is another duality; gate to learning the direct (mystic) experience, freeing one from the entanglement of a linear experience of time. There is nothing linear about nature. Linear time kills in many ways. Timelessness, eternity, is a common experience if one reflects on those experiences when time stood still, while you were in love vs. waiting for a P break.

Timelessness/Real time

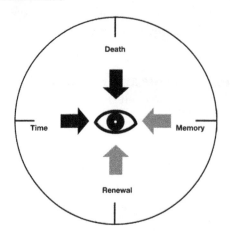

What black is to white, time is to timelessness, as memory is to forgetting.

Linear time meets memory at ground zero.

To beget the NEW.

As the eagle soars up in the sky, details get blurred.

But the essential is not lost,

It swoops down faster to the goal.

Knows when to strike and when to sail.

To switch between time and timelessness.

What to gather and to leave behind.

Complete the learning so as to forget.

Learn history so that history is created.

Both personal and collective, for the flow of life to go on.

Bury the dead so that renewal rules, not death and decay.

Free the ground for the dance of eternity—timelessness.

Habit/New habits

H armony
   appiness

A mor
   mrut

B eing
   ecoming

I ntelligence
   ntuition

T imelessness
   ransformation

Transcend habits with more powerful habits. Habit is history that keeps us stuck. Even death is a habit and fear of death is the mother of all fears that drives many businesses. Resistance creates resistance. If the child wants to touch fire we can tell her don't do it—a sure fire way of achieving what we never wanted. Instead show her the butterfly. Her attention is shifted to something beautiful. Big time improvement strategists play the latter game. They don't preach change. They play the game of radical improvement through which people come together as one, in relationships, internal and external alignment, creating history. In the process we move forward, get unstuck. Everyone wins and none loses.

Amor is the Roman god of love. The root from Sanskrit 'amar' means immortal and 'amrut' is that which makes one immortal—knowledge. Work is love expressed said Khalil Gibran. The path to immortality, exceptional performance, is possible only through transformation of work as an expression of the self, an expression of love.

Man meets Woman

Man meets woman, Adam and Eve

Since their parting outside the gates of paradise

They had lost their selves

At the beginning of time or even before

Together they saw the road they came

That they thought was the wrong one

Or was it the right one?

Why did he tell us not to eat from the tree of knowledge?

Now we know

He wanted us to eat from the tree, crafty old fox that he was

And continues no less to be

Now that the lesson is learnt the wrong one has become the right path

The pain gives way to a silent growing pleasure

Together they went back in time over the ages

Seeing how they were reduced to their shadows

Empty cages from which the parrots had escaped, long long ago

Now the parrot has come back to its nest

No more the cage that it thought it was

No more the parrots that they thought they were

But eagles waiting for the thermals

To take them up into the new sky over the blue oceans

The world will never be the same again.

The cloud community college

Continual learning is the path to continual renewal. Nature is in a process of continual renewal, but for the ecological footprints left by our interventions. It takes more than a year for nature to renew what we consume in a year and some damage is irreparable.

The frog in the well forms a model of the world. The eagle on the tree has a different model. When the frog is taken out by the eagle and brought back into the well, these two merge together to form a map of the world. The world has not changed but the models of the world have changed. We had a flat earth model in the not too distant past. With better technology and tools these models have given way to maps with increasing precision. Though maps of the physical world have become more precise, the mental models that went with them are not easily discarded.

The eagle represents the big picture and the frog the details. Both are connected just as the Hubble telescope sends us pictures from outer space and the Femtoscope helps us see the smallest of the small.

The eagle represents the global and the frog the local, which are but different perspectives of the whole. Thus being GLOCAL is an imperative. So is the imperative of continual learning, leading to continual renewal. We are frogs in the well of nature.

A brief history of learning/ renewal

Real work is the expression of a mature self.

As a dairy technologist, I used to watch the huge butter churns in motion, waiting for that magical moment when the cream breaks out into globules of butter. This was my first project at work—to find a solution to the mountains of cream that had accumulated over the previous surplus season. In the long hours that I worked towards reducing the bulk, I was forced to fight the boredom, visualising the mythical churning of the sea of milk by the Devas and Asuras to make amrit; the stuff that makes one immortal—knowledge.

Later on, I had the privilege of observing a very sedentary ascetic centenarian during the last 25 years of his pursuit of learning, which had started at the age of nine. At 60 he had made it known that he had another 40 years of work left to complete. He completed his 40 years and went on for another six months and 15 days.

In developed nations the fastest growing segment of the population is centenarians.

While most 'successful' people in the 'modern world' (read top of the pyramid!) contribute in real terms for 15/20 years of their life span of around 75, what goes into the making of the rare centenarian who remains productive many times over? If the product is in the process, what makes this process so rewarding in itself that it keeps them relatively less mortal physically and immortal in the world of knowledge. Why are we not able to go beyond them as a community?

A new scientific truth does not triumph by convincing its opponents and making them see the light, but rather because its opponents eventually die and a new generation grows up that is familiar with it, said Max Planck (1858-1947).

Imagine the churning that preceded the above statement!

Ever wondered about the history of churning and the consequences?

We have a secret dread of being thought ignorant. And we end by being ignorant after all, only we have done it in a long and roundabout way—from Rabindranath Tagore's (1861-1941) short story *Once there was a King*. His *The Parrot's Tale* develops this theme in much greater detail. Viswabharati, the university he set up, was the solution that he came up with for the problem.

There are only two ways to live: Either without thinking of death or with the thought that you approach death with every hour of your life, said Leo Tolstoy (1828-1910). There is, however, a third way—the path of regeneration, living with birth/death, NOW, in real time. The path taken by the high performing centenarians and the path open to the next generation who could go far beyond them. Most of us live in linear time. Living in real time is living in eternity.

Tolstoy was a prophets' prophet, a link in the long chain from Buddha, Ashoka the great and Christ who greatly influenced two of the heroes of our time and kept alive the idea of non-violence and non-action—Mohandas Karamchand Gandhi (1869-1948) and Martin Luther King, Jr (1929-1968).

Why do champions of non-violence die a violent death?

Tolstoy's thoughts on 'how to live', outlined in his *A Calendar of Wisdom*, appears to have founded the human potential movement much ahead of the new age messiahs. He died on his way to become a wandering ascetic. Imagine the churning.

Fyodor Mikhaylovich Dostoyevsky (1821-1881) turned out to be more prophetic than Tolstoy—Raskolnikov, the hero of *Crime and Punishment* is the template for our current role models who have perfected the art of committing the perfect crime and earning their place in history as saviours of the world.

The product is in the process

The seats of learning/churning/clashes and the interplay of history, knowledge, power, religion, politics and culture:

Taxila—6th century BCE to the 5th century CE

Nalanda—427 to 1197 CE

The Imperial Nanjing Institute, China—Founded in 258 CE, has perhaps the longest unbroken tradition.

Buddha, Christ, Ashoka—304 BCE-232 BCE; all belong to this period.

Taxila was burnt to ashes in 1197. The fire went on for weeks.

Prophet Mohammed—570-632 CE

The University of Al-Karaouine, Morocco—Founded in 859 CE by two wealthy sisters. It has played a leading role in cultural and academic relations between the Islamic world and Europe in the Middle Ages.

University of Bologna, Italy—Founded in the 12th century CE. The term university was coined at the founding of this seat of learning. The University of Paris, founded even earlier, was split into 13 universities in 1970.

University of Oxford, UK—The exact year of its formation is uncertain, but it has existed in some form since 1096 CE.

University of Cambridge, UK—1209 CE

The printing press—invented in 1440 CE

Martin Luther—lived from 1483 to 1546

Harvard University—1636

Karl Heinrich Marx—lived from 1818 to 1883

John Maynard Keynes—lived from 1883 to1946

W. Edwards Deming—lived from 1900 to 1993

Peter Ferdinand Drucker—lived from 1909 to 2005. Drucker had personal experience of the Nazi regime, probably would have listened to Sigmund Freud as a child and was a student of Keynes and Schumpeter. He foresaw the possibilities of the modern corporation and continuously reinvented himself. One might conclude that he also foresaw the need for a new paradigm of management with the focus on the self, managing oneself, for which he himself would remain one of the best models.

Drucker started the study of General Motors in 1945, leading to the publication of the *Concept of the Corporation* and began his career as a consultant, teacher and writer. For half a century, he remained at the forefront of the discipline he founded.

Deming started from where Drucker left-off. Had Deming been accepted in his home country as much as Drucker was in the country of his adoption, we perhaps wouldn't have been in our current crisis. The prophet is seldom respected at home. One could argue that Japan had the cultural pre-requisites to accept Deming and the US ultimately had to give in, reluctantly, to the competition. Drucker could not save the corporation/s whereas Deming left a legacy which forms the foundation for the discipline that Drucker is said to have founded.

The Internet—1992. The parrot leaves the cage, the seats of learning move to the clouds. The Internet has dematerialised learning from the seats of learning. Technology has become real time, but people are yet to move to real time. We need new paradigms to bridge the gaps and transcend the learning plateaus in our journey of continual renewal and improvement.

A new discipline and pedagogy—The First Discipline

Is the discipline of sustained high performance.

Context—The BRIC is broken; The tail wags the head; WMD—destruction or dialogue? War on terror/for talent—WFT; Dream merchants and the revenge of the underdogs—Liberation of talent; Recession, booms and busts, the long cycles and the bubbles in between; Is there a future? The rise or fall of India, Indian=Global; The climate/energy crisis, water/food security and sustainability; Finance capital, Human capital, Community capital, Ecosystem management, Developmental management, Rethinking development and governance; Reinventing the discipline of management

Management Overview—Missing the wood for the trees; What we failed to see, Marketing Myopia, Theodor Levitt, Peter Drucker, The Bystander, End of economic man to managing oneself; Beyond competitive advantage

First Discipline, SHPC—A map to the future and the road ahead:

Continual Renewal, regeneration therapy

Personal mastery and LLL (Life Long learning), learning plateaus

System/s thinking

Accelerated learning and mental maps, knowledge management

Positioning yourself, your business for SHP

Community intelligence

The singularity perspective—the map of all maps

The Practice of First Discipline—The tool kit, a backpack for the road; Dialogue and storytelling; Analytics and gap analysis; Aligning with the deep structure; Conscious dreaming; Participative action learning, research and real time management development; Sustained high performance—growth by design.

Custodians of the Future—The blue ocean people; milk is white; God's own country, devil's too—between the devil and the deep sea; the ecosystem people, fishermen/ tribal communities; fusion fuel and the energy challenge.

Creating a Future by Design—Rethinking CSR, wealth and charity

Strategy—Animating the learning engine, maintaining the LE for SHP

Appendix—The context for First Discipline: The global failure of management as a discipline, Enron to Lehman brothers, recession, failure of IT, bubbles, poverty and conflicts. Thought leaders; Peter Drucker over the years. In spite of all the hype, management in the west also has failed to deliver in the global context.

Local failures:

- Failure to connect to the developmental management issues of India.

- Failure to define what is Indian (global) about management.

- Failure to attract management to governance and development.

- Academic work in India has failed to make a global impact.

- A dialogue between an academic and a development practitioner.

- The collapse of governance.

- The disillusionment with managers and academics, failure of leadership/intellectualism.

- The majority are left to fend for themselves.

Technology and access in a connected world—One man can make a difference. IT was entrepreneurial/technological/learning breakthrough and not a product of management thought.

These issues remain to be further explored through this dialogue; issue such as:

- Competencies of the new manager—A development practitioner?

- Birth of the professional manager: the ethical/competency/ community imperatives

- Peter Drucker vs. Amartya Sen

- Stafford Beer vs. Peter M. Senge

- Prahlad vs. Porter

- Chris Argyris vs. Maslow—End of the organisation man?

- Deming vs. Drucker

- Aurobindo vs. Ken Wilbur

- Management development, nurturing the new managers

- Action learning—Reginald Revans

- Schumacher vs. Schumpeter

- Kuhn

Free will and the immortality quotient

Ideas are like antibiotics. They lose their potency over time.

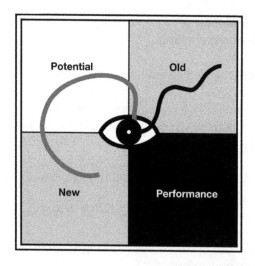

Resistant/mutant versions of bacteria or viruses surface and the search for more potent ones adds to our 'busy-ness', a Pandora's Box. Intelligence would have been an appropriate term to discuss what we are about to. Intelligence has become intelligences like one God in the west becomes many in the east. There are too many shades and versions of them. We too have contributed to the babble. Community and gender intelligence are our favourite buzzwords in this dialogue.

So what is the new coinage? Why is it imperative?

There are many reasons. The first one is semantic. We talk about change, change is the only constant and so on. Change can be +ve or -ve. The +ve and -ve might cancel each other out or what we now think +ve may be -ve in the long run.

We talk in such gross generalities that the word is killed and the talk only adds to the noise pollution. Our communication has no power. The word does not create and it is like a mantra chanted ad nauseum, without understanding its meaning. Had we been talking about improvement in place of change, we would have been far better off.

Let us take a resolution that change is out and improvement is in.

Another one is our preoccupation with the immediate, the quarterly, playing Robin Hood and robbing Peter to pay Paul, quick fixes that kill even the remote possibility of sustained or sustainable improvement. If we are driven by the logic of the marketplace and the best sellers, we will always be after a mirage; this format would not be necessary and no dialogue will be possible. We need a core of permanence, the centre, to accumulate the pearl material. The best sellers are designed to be best sellers and the best of them are the result of some intelligent repackaging. This is what intelligence has come to.

Now that we have many an example of Skill+killings and Layings, (read Enron and the rest of the list) we know what the best and the most intelligent are and what the war for talent has come to be.

Why are we tagging immortality with free will?

Free will is about choice, whether to be an angel of death or a devil for life. The immortality option is seldom explored because we are bogged down by the burden of normality, which has nothing to do with true normality. To conform is natural yet not 'natural'.

To be immortal is to stand the test of time. The blue ocean people are pointers in this direction. Buddha, Christ and Mohammed continue to be immortal and alive to influence our dominant worldviews. It is not really a clash of civilisations, but a clash between mortals and immortals. With longer life spans and the late bloomers, we are about to face challenges of relative physical immortality and eventually the problems of physical immortality.

It is better to believe in life/immortality and die a physical death due to any number of possible causes, than to believe in death and die before physical death.

Do we really believe in free will?

We may not but we would like to. An ounce of prevention is better than all the cures. We pretend that we have free will because we want to live in free will while we continue to freewheel, like we pretend that we are working or adding value while we add to the semantic confusion, noise pollution and kill more trees. We don't see evidence of anything free in the real sense of the term and it seems like the proverbial 'eternal recurrence'.

It is a problem of what we pay attention to. We see brief manifestations of free will when we look at improvements over time and cumulatively we have many things to be put in perspective to build up a case for free will.

It could be our resolution that we will work hard to develop a little of it.

So be it.

Religion owes its origin to immortality. "I will always be with you till the end," said Christ. For 'Peters', the managers, institutional and personal self-interest take precedence over the conceptual and the visionary. Dependence is the fuel for survival of the pyramids. Hierarchic religion will be the first casualty of empowerment!

How do you select a facilitator, guru or even your physician, the consultant?

If you meet the Buddha on the road, kill him. There are no Buddhas any more.

Henry Mintzberg says: "Coach ourselves." Gurus die very young.

If the emperor claims to be the emperor, he is no emperor.

We are in transition to the age of the common Buddha. If you are in doubt, check it up at the corner shop.

Let us bury the dead. Shun the angels of death not the devils of life. Is she healthy physically, mentally, spiritually? Does she believe in community and dialogue? Is she an adult on the path to immortality? Does she see the adult in you, even if it is a dormant one? What is her IQ, immortality quotient, commitment to the long term?

In 1990, Tara was attending the beginners programme in yoga. The centre was part of a large international network. She was carried away by the 'presence' of the facilitator and at the end of the sessions wanted to remain in touch with him. In the twenty sessions that they worked together with around twenty participants he had never shared his name or any other details. She was curious and once the question popped out of her.

"How old are you?'

"I am ageless."

"May I know your name?"

"What is in a name?"

This was all the one to one conversation that she had. She continues to practise yoga. She returned to the centre more than once in search of the guru who had set her on her yogic path. He had left the centre and they could not help her trace him. But memories and the learning remain. His words to the group still echo in her: "All learning is in the body. The body is the learning engine."

What is in a name?

Pied Pipers?

Ratsinger

Zuckerberg, it sucks

The millions averaging six hours a day

It sucks, is it social?

Bill Gates and Windows

Open the windows, Close the Gates

Do a Mother Teresa

End of Strategy!

Obama, Osama, the double or the other?

Bush and ambush, plain vanilla bush

Schwarzkopf and shotskop

Friedman, hot, flat, crowded and fried?

Hawking, hawks?

Grand design

Or Grand default?

Satyam=truth, Adarsh=the ideal

Maytas, truth reinvented the Indian way

Just two from the Indian summer of scams

Skill+Killings, spice it with Layings

Enron follows and the others join

Mc Kinsey, Donalds and WhartOn All!

Hamel's hammer?

So much for the talent hunt

What a hunt?

What a war?

Overdogs or underdogs

What do the dogs see?

Outliers or mainstream

Black swans or White,

All is not well in Gladwell's well

Where the eagles do not dare

Connect the dots, says he

Patterns, puzzles, mysteries and the misery

It is a mystic mandala

Hi Charles

It is very Handy

To be appropriately selfish

Read Will

Durant the durable

Not the perishables

The case for India

He had something of free will

Not a free wheeler

For a taste of your own medicine

Appropriate selfishness

Stay Hungry, Stay foolish

Says the richest from the pulpit

Wow, what a Job, Connect the dots

Echoes Bansal from the land of immortals

Meluha

The empty raincoat, making sense of the future

Let us make sense of the present

The future will take care of itself

Empty drums echo best

The new Brahmins

Brahmin=Knowledge bearer, Vidyadhara

Vidya=real knowledge

Vidyadhara=one who bears knowledge

Vidya was lost on the way

Knowledge bearers became plain bearers

A country went under

History repeats on other shores

Connect the Dots, Manuel

God is with us

Will the elephant dance?

Will it?

Wont it?

We Will

Free will and freewheel.

Angels of death and devils of life, old and new

What would you prefer to be, an angel of death or a devil of life? Be a devil of life, a ruthless one at that, 8x5 if not 24x7.

If the belief in god begets the devil, isn't it better not to believe in that god? God and devil, life and death need not be at the poles and in opposition to create each other. If charity begets charity, it takes a lot of courage to stop being charitable.

Can life die? Everything that lives eventually dies, says a popular author to his six year old son who asks, 'will our sun eventually die and the earth turn into a lifeless planet?' It takes some understanding and even more courage to say, 'I don't know'.

The true scientist working to decipher the code for biological immortality has no option but to take a different position, live that reality at least in part, now. For her, life never dies, everything that lives need not necessarily die. She chooses to pay attention to 'facts' to support her position and work towards translating the dream to a lived reality all through her living life. She sees everything alive and not dying. She too could die, but she truly lived when she lived out of the shadow of death. Biological immortality is a virtual reality for her, now.

Nature continually renews itself. We create death working overtime, resisting nature. Our best selling author also does almost the same, paying attention to 'facts' to support his position, spreading the message of death all through his dying life. Death is the virtual reality for him now. The coward dies many deaths.

The author is an angel of death and the scientist, a devil of life. A devil of life is rarer than a black swan.

Black swans are exceptions when we take very thin slices of time and space. Compare this with the universal, all slices of time and space. Imagine all the unknown earths where white swans are as rare as black swans are on our planet. In some future time we would be 'successful' in making white swans extinct so that the black swans will be the normality. Or, it could also be true that in 'her-story' in some unknown past, nobody wrote a 'his-story' of the swans; black swans were the normality. America was doing all right, perhaps better from some other perspective, even before Columbus! Thanks to Nassim Nicholas Taleb for the trigger, a black swan in our present slice of time and space. In the cacophony of the marketplace, the one with the best noise box is listened to and being audacious is integral to a b-school education. One is advised to have big, hairy, audacious goals. We go to great lengths to prove that we belong to 'mediocristan' to use one of Taleb's coins. Mediocristan and extremistan are two sides of the same coin which has a third side for ordinary mortals like us and many more sides for the likes of Taleb, which most students, and their professors, fail to connect to in their case studies in b-school. In the medium run all of us are dead or 'fooled' in mediocristan, the flat land.

Angels of death come in all colours and shades, most pleasing, gentle, dying to do good, promising to make you all powerful, beautiful, immortal, a full life here, another one after your death—'mutually inclusive', so on and so forth. The cosmetics peddler, medicine man, philanthropist, priest, pedagogues, top of the pyramid, blue chip performance, pied pipers, astrologers, snake oil in all rainbow colours . . . noblest of intentions. The effect is invariably malignant and they are so sure of themselves. You will never hear them say, 'I do not know'. We are not that sure.

The devils of life come in grey. They are very rare. Keep searching. Appearances are very very deceptive. There could be a beginners' dilemma.

Keep paying attention to the new. Everything is renewed. Life never dies. Somewhere on the way, the tipping point will come, death will be the abnormal and life the normal. Biology will be more in fashion than Physics.

Why wait for the prophet who will never come? Let us begin building our ark.

We become what we pay attention to. Resistance creates resistance. Do not resist. Meera looks at the jaded jeans from her b-school days, completing a quarter century of companionship. She chooses to see the new feel of it, today, now.

Positioning: Where are we?

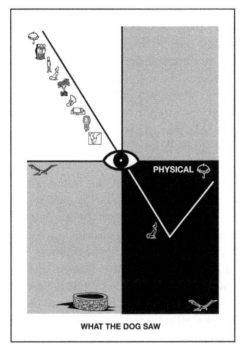

WHAT THE DOG SAW

What the dog sees and we don't. Who has gone aSTRAY? "From the lowly perspective of a dog's eyes, everyone looks short,"—Chinese proverb.

IF

Just as we forget phone numbers and multiplication tables thanks to cell phone memories and calculators, we have forgotten to check our positions and some whiz-kid has hacked into all the GPSs to show the wrong position

THEN

We will all be rushing madly to where no one really wants to go

WHAT IF

This is the truth with or without GPS?

The corruption in our thinking is at the very source itself!

So how do we debug the source code?

For us, the dog's is a lowly perspective. But we can prove that the dog's position is above us and ours is the lowly perspective. All dogs do not see the same. Stray dogs see even better than their domesticated fellows. The latter become less intelligent in the process of socialisation with the humans who cut them to size to suit their unfulfilled needs and wants of relationships and community. We are far inferior to them on community intelligence and I have reasons to conclude that the stray dogs see that we have gone astray! This is what the visual above shows.

The top left quadrant shows the increasing potential of simple to complex systems. The bottom right quadrant shows the corresponding performance at each level of systems. We don't see a gap between potential and performance till the level of animals, the level which also includes dogs. From the level of animals we see a fall, which we take as great progress. What we see depends on where we stand. In the case of the human and still higher systems, performance is below that of animals. The fall is so steep that it is just on par with simple systems similar to a clock. What we see as great progress is a myth and we are firing on all cylinders heading towards disaster without even realising it.

Where are we? We encountered Chandrasekhar, a friend of mine, in an earlier story. As we saw then, I found him one morning in front of his regular bar, frantic and searching for a familiar face. He wanted to go home, but he didn't know where he was. Imagine his relief to meet me. He could not hold on and it just popped out of him: "Where am I?" He was greatly relieved. I was not. It continues to haunt me that we know far more about the unreachable stretches of space than what is closest to us and we go around creating a world outside to take the garbage inside us. That also includes the cosmologist who attributes his fear of death to the universe, seeing it breaking down like a clock.

The position and positions—Without answering where we are as a species, we cannot have an answer to 'where am I' as an individual.

The first step to a common journey, to go home or elsewhere, virtual or otherwise, is to know where we are now. The GPS or the compass eases our regular journeys. Progress is a different kind of a journey and we are yet to agree on this first step. Each of us has a different position on this and the proverbial babble of Babel is the corollary. When we have different positions it is imperative that our perspectives do not converge. Unless we agree on a non-controversial reference to the starting point there will be no common journey.

When our basic assumptions about the home position, the reference point, are wrong it is certain that we will reach some place where we never wanted to go. Any process of improvement calls for fixing a starting position, deciding on the direction and reflecting/reviewing with reference to the starting position.

For a moment let us take position where the four lines meet and take in the common perspective that collectively we are no better than a clock in terms of our performance against our collective potential to perform.

Now it becomes possible to fix a direction for improvement and on this journey of improvement there will be variant positions as we move forward.

Now it is also possible to position myself (example: a professional or a facilitator to the journey) and see the variant positions, milestones, on that long journey.

Blue Ocean People at the Top of the Pyramid, BOP@TOP

Potentially, any one of us could aspire to be one of them. The Wiki 'list of lists' of centenarians will give you a feel of what I have in mind. Most of the people on that list would qualify to be on the BOP@TOP list that I am compiling.

Having worked for over three decades at the bottom of the pyramid and branded myself a low impact lifer, aka poor, much before the jargon was in vogue, I am more fascinated with people at the top of the pyramid; the BOP@TOP that is. It is for the TOP to make it lighter for those at the bottom. We have enough of them to show us that it is indeed possible. These people have taken the road less, or not, travelled. They show us the direction of the journey, milestones that point to further stretches of the road not taken, of the unrealised, unexplored territories, the blue ocean space of strategic directions for self-management or HRM, human resources management, to use b-school jargon. They give much more than they take. They are low impact on inputs and very high impact on output. They bridge us with the past and point to us the future.

175

For me HRM is Hira Ratan Manek. Born in 1937, a graduate in mechanical engineering who carried on with the family business of shipping and spice trading till he retired in 1992. After working for 3 years, he re-discovered the secrets of sun gazing. Since 18 June 1995 HRM has lived only on sun energy and water. Occasionally he drinks tea, coffee and buttermilk. He had three strict fasts during which he had just sun energy and only water and was under the control and observation of various scientific and medical teams. The first of these fasts lasted for 211 days which was followed by a 411-day fast from 2000-2001 in Ahmedabad. Indeed it is written: "Man shall not live by bread alone."

Another one is Pandit Sudhakar Krishna Rao Chaturvedi, a vedic scholar, teacher, writer, translator and journalist who was born in 1897. At 113+ years, he says it is said in the Vedas that a person of pure character can live for 300 years. He hopes to live that long. He has planned his work for another ten years.

P. C. Devassia, who I knew from up close for over two decades and have talked about earlier in this book, lived for 100 years, 6 months and 15 days. This by itself is not a feat, but how those years were spent is. On the day he retired from nearly four decades of work, he talked about how he planned to spend his remaining 40 years. All those forty years were exceptionally productive, even more productive than the first forty years of work. His magnum opus, *Kristubhagavatam*, a meeting point of two cultures was written in his 70s. The decision to live for a 100 years was a conscious one taken very early in life; the direction was set and reflection was a continuous process. His work was his spirituality and he was religious about it. Making work meaningful and fun is the best medicine to live long. Instead, we wait for a day when nano-robots will make it possible for us to become immortal.

Dominic Chacko Kizhkemuri, DC, was born in 1914. He worked as a teacher for over a decade, was involved in the freedom struggle and imprisoned and promoted SPCS—the writers' cooperative which created history. He retired at the age of 60 and started his own publishing firm DC Books, with a capital of less than $200, which became a market leader in the business by the time he died in 1999.

I am grateful to my b-school education for introducing to me many of the following lighthouse people. Some of them continue to be beacons for us and would qualify to be included in the list of immortals if there were one.

The immortality quotient, my fascination for the long term, was triggered by them:

W. Edwards Deming—1900-1993

Ludwig von Bertalanffy—1901-1972

William Ross Ashby—1903-1972

Peter F. Drucker—1909-2005

Kenneth E. Boulding—1910-1993

Russell L. Ackoff—1919-2009

Anthony Stafford Beer—1926-2002

Ronald Coase—1910-2013

Emanuel Revici, M.D.—1896-1998

Obviously, living a long life is not the only qualifier to be on the list of BOP@TOP. Warren Buffet or Bill Gates will not qualify in spite of the combined weight of their charities.

The Blue Ocean Strategy, W. Chan Kim and Rene Mauborgne's book, is about uncontested market space; how market leaders continue to stay far ahead of the competition without wasting their energy and effort on market wars. I draw my lessons from people, not corporates, having lost my faith in b-schools and business after my four years of education in two of them.

Imagine the vast unexplored space that is available to move on and the spin offs if more of us decide to adopt a blue ocean strategy in our lives. That would set one of the coordinates for strategic HRM. The blue ocean space that each individual discovers around oneself is the major driver for growth and improvement, true of all of history and the drive behind all those in the *Guinness World Records*. The future is in the making when we see this collective blue ocean space that remains unexplored.

The seniors shall inherit the earth, but can one grow old and young at the same time?

Some people, a small minority, do it. They mature like old whisky and still remain young, challenging common wisdom that old dogs cannot pick up new tricks. For some seniors growing old and growing young are parallel processes. They challenge their brain with continual learning. The result, plasticity of the brain improves. Intelligence too has the same character. It improves if one keeps challenging it against problems. When the brain remains young and one is driven by work that is motivating on its own merit, the body grows young, renewing itself continually like a river which is not blocked from renewal by our ecological footprints. One grows old and young at the same time.

Olive Riley, once the world's oldest blogger, passed away at 108. She must have picked up blogging when quite old by our usual standards. I also know some very smart, much younger people who boast of not using the Internet or the computer claiming that they are against too much technology. I am afraid it is a camouflage to cover up the resistance to embrace the new. In my search for the old and young, I met Joseph Smith. He weathered many a storm on the high seas and on land for 82 years and graduated from the school of hard knocks. He is old and young, more active and concerned than most of us about the way the system works or does not. The 'old and young' need closer attention because they are travelling a different road, which is likely to be a mega trend, gathering momentum.

Elsewhere, there is a conversation going on about the future of social enterprise. I am convinced that the future of business is in the enhancement of community, global and local. I believe that every business, including the business of religion and non-profits, is about creating community within to connect to the community outside and business performance ought to be measured by the enhancement of community or net value addition to the community capital. Many businesses, very successful by conventional norms, could be destroying community. They survive and grow by reinforcing the business of shadows and substitutes. Growth does not differentiate between real goods and services and shadows and substitutes.

Established religions have stood the test of time, but have a shadow side to their existence. They appear to be more successful than most business organisations in promising the most intangible with the lowest cost of production, manipulating masses on the fear of death and retribution in next life. Priests and politicians play God and peddle dependence. Many of them love to be worshipped and are on a drive to fulfil their own power drive distortions. Did someone say that the earth will be revealed to us when heaven is destroyed?

Will insurance companies have any business if people have no fear of death or the future? If people are anchored to their true SELVES how would the fashion and cosmetics business, which often assumes that the cosmetic is more important than the content, respond?

Would there be a fall in demand for big screen heroes if we reframe our notions of the hero to the real meaning of the term—conquering one's own fear?

If people redefine work as self-expression, will they continue to suffer from boredom and, consequently, will the market for entertainment products and services shrink? The entertainment industry stretches itself to keep boredom at bay. The demand is a derived one from the inability to find a purpose in life and work that is motivating by itself.

How would lotteries and the stock market fare if more people put an end to the 'wait for a better day' game and start living in the present?

More than economics, distorted human drives drive the economy. Which business is not a social enterprise though most of them implicitly admit that they are antisocial. What would be the role of charity—other than as a measure of guilt associated with wealth—when every business redefines its mission as enhancing global community?

These are landscapes that one might come across on the two roads, one by design and the other by default.

One can go on ad nauseum about the shadow side of every business, profit or non-profit. I believe more than religions, business will take the road to spirituality. I have experienced better community in business than in religious organisations. Business will be more pressed to reinvent itself as enhancing community within, to connect better to the external community locally and globally in a borderless world.

It is not easy for businesses or individuals to walk out of the shadows, because we will have to turn against our own vested interests, the shadow side.

The 'young and old' show the way. The most successful of them have no learning plateaus as they take their positions very early in life. They quit only when their mission is fulfilled. The others have successfully negotiated the learning plateaus at different stages of their life. They live a life of their own design and they are their own heroes. They earn credibility with their life and walk the talk. They are not looking for a secure tenure or driven by the need to perform in the marketplace where your future is as volatile as the stock market; where, in the first 15 years of your career, your fate is almost sealed whether you are 'top of the pyramid' material or not. Demography favours the seniors. Thanks to the Web, more of them are finding their voice and we have enough of them in the public domain to listen to and learn from on how to live a life by design.

The elephant-rock declaration—In one of our workouts, twelve 60+ couples, got together to discuss the trend, climbed the elephant rock and shouted out the elephant rock declaration: "The seniors shall inherit the earth."

Dialogues—Aging out of life

Meenakshi asks, "In our time, do we age out of life?"

Like most questions, the answers are yes, no and yes and no.

"Death is not essential," said the Mother. Reading this, has been a milestone in my learning.

Life begins when we resolve our issues with death and ageing. We are not designed to die but to live. Death is a habit and we are breaking more and more out of this habit—people are living longer.

What is time? Is it linear, one-way traffic, an arrow that moves from birth to death?

This cannot be natural since nothing in nature is linear. There is an arrow of time that goes in the opposite direction; memory, how we RE-collect our past. The sun we see is around 9 minutes old, but our thought does not take nine minutes to reach the sun we see, the sun that was nine minutes ago.

Yes, thought is faster than light.

As we talk our cells die and new cells are born; two more arrows, to put it in a very crude way. In place of the first arrow, we have four arrows of time now.

When this is experienced, birth and death become simultaneous, not a journey from point A to B or birth to death. One transcends linear time and steps into eternity, becoming ageless.

So we age out of linear time, not out of life and start living in the NOW—eternity.

When was I born? MM-DD-YYYY? That was the birth of my body.

Did I have anything to do with it?

The real me was born much later when I RE-collected all that scattered stuff and put it all together and walked out of the shadows of death, linear time, my unconscious. I then took that first step to the birth of myself, eternity and continual renewal.

How old are you?

I have multiple choices to suit the questioner:

I am 64, for the straights.

I am 39 when I count from the birth of my SELF.

I am 29 if I count from when I decided to live life on my terms (It took ten years for the self to become mature enough to make that decision).

15 billion years, in arrow terms.

The logic is that I am as old as the Universe and everything that went on is mapped in me in many ways.

> 15 billion years—something in me will go on living forever.

< 2 years—the age of the oldest cell in my body.

Take your pick or all of it.

Have some more of your own answers.

It is always better to have as many answers, perspectives, than any one single answer.

NAN

What is NAN? The Indian bread? New Age Nonsense?

Well, I could have died yesterday. I haven't. What greater miracle do you need to make life wonderful?

So what is the answer, without beating around the bush?

In 'our times' we can age out of time itself.

We can age out of life too.

It is a Choice.

Building our ark; living in real time

In the beginning was the word and before the beginning, we lived in real time.

Most of us live in linear time and some in real time. Those living in real or relative, real time live longer, the blue ocean people. Those living in linear time die early.

Noah, Aaron and Abner are children from my neighbourhood. It is fascinating why we go back to the Old Testament to dig up these names? History and myths chase us when we don't understand them . . .

Books can be written only in linear time. So also history. In real time, all of the past and all of future are NOW. From now, we connect to a history of the future.

In linear time we and the world were born at some distant past. We and the world will die in some far away future.

The Wright brothers were right; they gave expression to our collective longing to fly. Buddha, Christ, Mohammed and Gandhi voiced our longing to break free in a different way. We played with technology to break free from the confines of the planet driven by some distant memories of longer flights. In the beginning was oneness and the longing for oneness took us to transcending the barriers of time and space. With the emergence of the Web and the cloud, when we are stuck in the clouds for hours we have a semblance of what it is to live in real time.

In real time the flood is now, not in some distant past. It calls for all our skills to craft an ark to survive the flood. One such skill is to transcend the linear to dynamic and real time. The ark is the symbol of the self. Everything of the past is embedded in it, a new synthesis of all that has happened in the past, the sum of all improvements in the evolutionary journey, plants, animals and a select few from the millions who are ready for the transformational voyage, crafting an accumulator to collect everything with a survival value and stepping into a new future of rainbow promises.

The old fisherman took me to the shore and pointed to the horizon, some distant waves and the shoal. I could not see any fish. I pretended that I could, the coward that I was. Then on, I started watching the waves and learnt to see beyond the waves. Gradually it fell in place, how all the waves—tangible and intangible—come together to create what we create.

It is against our programming to think in waves. Unlike fishermen, men on land have come to think in straight lines which leads us to booms and busts rather than waves and cycles which are but natural. But we are always taken by surprise. The captains could not see beyond the linear, the waves and cycles.

Dev complains that the dialogue brushes past too many issues and leaves every one of them unexplained.

Dialogue is for ADULTs. They need no advice. You can at best draw their attention or perhaps provoke them to ask questions. Once this is achieved they need be left to make the rest of the connections (If there are gaps one can always Google it). There has to be enough space for the adult to find itself and mature.

Now that the context is set and the flood is more than a myth, the choice is between building your own ark or a community one. The latter happens only in myths and is beyond our scope.

There is no substitute to building a personal one. We need as many arks as possible rather than waiting for another Noah. Each one needs to build an ark for oneself. Without learning to ride the waves, one cannot lend a helping hand. That would be catalysing suicide

The pyramids were built when the valley was fertile and the soil supported the community. The floods used to keep the soil fertile. When we were young, we celebrated the floods which were a rare event. It was a time for joy, taking out the canoes and frolicking in the water. Now they have built embankments on the river. When the river swells, the currents are stronger, digging the bottom of the river further down. The embankments get washed away, but are strengthened continuously, further accelerating the death of the river. The forests were replaced by a wide portfolio of crops that more or less acted like natural forests, which then gave way to the plantations, fertilisers, pesticides and weedicides. Now the soil is dying. Floods, when they come, spread the pesticides and weedicides all over, further accelerating the rot.

The other flood is more difficult to see. The most endangered species is the Homo Sapiens and not the others on the list. History tells us that the collapse takes more than 100 years for the full cycle to be completed. When our span of attention is less than 15 years, we fail to see the flooding that takes a century or more.

The crisis could be the birth pangs of a new species. Nature is ruthless when it comes to the survival of the fittest.

One of the participants in a FD workshop had this dream of the Pied Piper and the giant wheel. We get onto the giant wheel and the operator decides when we need to get off. The music is so enchanting that we merrily join the flow, the flood. We become the frog soup, drowned in the flood.

We either dream of a glorious past or a glorious future. Neither helps; the flood/ crisis is a perennial one taking place here and now. We pray to our father who art in heaven. Just as we push him up (push HER underground) out of our lives, we dream of a golden past or a future. This is the problem with stimulus selectivity. We would like to listen to our favourite music and shut out the inconvenient and the unpleasant, out of focus.

Am I suggesting that we don't wait to save the planet, but be selfish enough to save our own skin. That may be the best that one can do, be appropriately selfish; I am reminded of Charles Handy.

Nature will see to it that in spite of floods and plagues there is enough left for the show to continue. One can choose which fork to take. The crowd will always be at least 20+ years behind the lone walker. Nobody is going to build a Lexus reading *The Toyota Way*.

We can learn from the people on the edge. The African proverb, a favourite of Al Gore and quoted in *Hot, Flat and Crowded* by Friedman: "If you want to go quickly go alone, but if you want to go far, go together," may at times turn out to be suicidal.

For Galileo it was much longer. Had he gone with the crowd, we wouldn't have him in the history books. The crowd and the pyramid dwellers took a long long time to reconcile with his personal vision. One cannot always go with the crowd. One has to learn to hunt with the hound as well as run with the hares.

What about the gurus, best sellers, the secret, the law of attraction, the self-improvement industry, NAN?

There are enough saviours/pied pipers who promise salvation. The crutches help till you learn to walk. Once you have learnt to walk, it is time to dump the crutches and listen to the guru inside. One cannot see through the other's eyes. We need new eyes to see a new vision NOW to create a desirable future.

Building the ark

What is the visual about?

The new eye, window to the self, reality.

We have attempted to map, create a visual of what we have been discussing. Perhaps one could meditate on it for some time. We were talking about the ark as the learning engine.

The ark is the learning engine that continually outperforms, beyond booms and busts, floods, feasts/festivals. It is about our self and selves.

More stories

We also use many of the following leads as triggers to facilitate the process during our workshops. It is for the facilitator to gauge the need of the participants and what is appropriate to the context:

What is your call?:http://en.wikipedia.org/wiki/ Lighthouse_and_naval_vessel_urban_legend

Blindness, Jose Saramago: http://en.wikipedia.org/wiki/ Jos%C3%A9_Saramago

Magister Ludi, Herman Hesse: http://en.wikipedia.org/wiki/Hermann_Hesse

The 100th monkey effect: http://en.wikipedia.org/wiki/Hundredth_monkey_effect

Blind men and the elephant: http://en.wikipedia.org/wiki/Blind_men_and_an_elephant

Don't shoot the messenger: http://en.wikipedia.org/wiki/Shooting_the_messenger

Mahabali and Vamana: http://en.wikipedia.org/wiki/Vamana

The imperial chill, Daniel Quinn: http://en.wikipedia.org/wiki/Daniel_Quinn

The Decision Compass

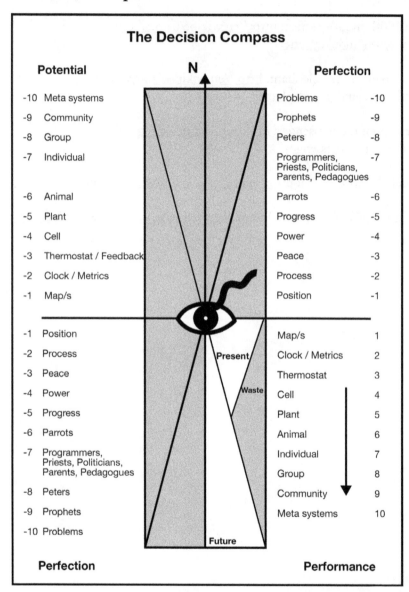

The Decision Compass

Potential		N		Perfection	
-10	Meta systems			Problems	-10
-9	Community			Prophets	-9
-8	Group			Peters	-8
-7	Individual			Programmers, Priests, Politicians, Parents, Pedagogues	-7
-6	Animal			Parrots	-6
-5	Plant			Progress	-5
-4	Cell			Power	-4
-3	Thermostat / Feedback			Peace	-3
-2	Clock / Metrics			Process	-2
-1	Map/s			Position	-1
-1	Position		Present	Map/s	1
-2	Process			Clock / Metrics	2
-3	Peace			Thermostat	3
-4	Power		Waste	Cell	4
-5	Progress			Plant	5
-6	Parrots			Animal	6
-7	Programmers, Priests, Politicians, Parents, Pedagogues			Individual	7
-8	Peters			Group	8
-9	Prophets			Community	9
-10	Problems		Future	Meta systems	10
Perfection				**Performance**	

"All the insights, noble thoughts, and works of art that the human race has produced in its creative eras, all that subsequent periods of scholarly study have reduced to concepts and converted into intellectual values, the Glass Bead Game player plays like the organist on an organ. And this organ has attained an almost unimaginable perfection; its manuals and pedals range over the entire intellectual cosmos; its stops are almost beyond number."—Herman Hesse

We work with limited information, knowledge and much less of wisdom. Though we have great faith in our decisions and they are invariably taken with the very best of intentions, most of them turn out to be not very wise. Which is where the Decision Compass comes in.

It is a tool that enables the user to appreciate the complexity of the decision making process and to improve outcomes in terms of quality, sustainability and community. It reduces the search effort involved in managerial problem solving, points to the solution space (blue ocean), accelerates learning and brings the woods and the trees together, without either perspective being lost.

The tool and methodology evolved across two decades, in the context of working with very challenging developmental issues and communicating these issues to diverse stakeholders.

The game itself: The Decision Compass is at the apex of a series of frames that together form the First Discipline Framework.

Mastery of the Decision Compass frame is achieved through accelerated learning and competency development workshops that simulate a high performance work environment. The participants work together (play), with specific roles corresponding to the levels and functional expectancies of the Decision Compass.

The game's duration ranges from 16 to 40 working hours across two to five days for an introductory workshop. The duration also varies based on the level of the participants and the mix of the facilitation team. There can be up to 50-60 participants in the game.

The First Discipline Framework is broken into its component frames across 60 coloured cards in the VIBGYOR spectrum. There are six Red cards and four Green cards, with 10 cards each of the other colours. Red and Green represent governance and sustainability issues and are external to the organisation, while the five other colours stand for various groups/teams within the organisation. The five organisational groups represent the corporate team at the centre and other teams, with one in each of the quadrants. Groups change positions anti-clockwise after each round of discussion and presentations, and with the change in positions the focus of each group also varies corresponding to its position.

Round 1:

Step 1—Pre process metrics

Step 2—The facilitators explain the Decision Compass (60 minutes)

Step 3—Each participant picks a card. In case the total number of participants is less than 60, some of them may have more than one card. These participants will perform the additional roles implied by the extra cards. Each participant on his/her own prepares and presents a brief note on his/her understanding of his/her role. The facilitators provide clarifications if necessary. As the process picks up, the extent of facilitation comes down (45-60 minutes).

Step 4—Participants form groups based on the colour of the card(s) they hold and assume their roles. They work towards connecting the learning from the exercise and its strategic implications. Presentations follow at hourly intervals. Further clarifications are provided by the facilitators at the end of each presentation (4-5 hours).

Step 5—Post metrics: At the end, the learning from Round 1 is summed up and shared. Further briefings happen, with organisational data or using data from sample case studies.

Round 2:

Step 1—The groups work with organisation-specific or case study-related information to demonstrate the application of the model and the implications.

Step 2—Summing up

Step 3—Post metrics

Additional rounds will be required in the case of new recruits. The rounds are repeated till the facilitators are certain that participants have reached the required level of proficiency as reflected by the metrics, quality of the presentations and proficiency with the language of sustained high performance.

Go to market strategies

"I am alive."

"No. I am anti-fragile," says Taleb.

"Hare and the tortoise," says a fable.

"Fast and slow, System A and B," says Daniel Kahneman.

"Which way to run," asks Ratsinger.

Suggested reading

Marketing Metaphoria: What Deep Metaphors Reveal about the Minds of Consumers—Gerald Zaltman and Lindsay Zaltman, HBS Press 2008.

http://blogs.scientificamerican.com/guest-blog/2010/07/27/of-two-minds-listener-brain-patterns-mirror-those-of-the-speaker/

The Power of Storytelling—Jim Holtje, Prentice Hall Press

The Leader's Guide to Storytelling—Stephen Denning, Jossey-Bass

Tell to Win—Peter Guber, Crown Business

Resonate—Nancy Duarte, John Wiley & Sons

Storybranding—Jim Signorelli, Greenleaf Book Group

Winning the Story Wars—Jonah Sachs, HBS Press

Illustrators and Visual Storytellers Map the World—Maria Popova

http://www.brainpickings.org/index.php/2013/03/07/a-map-of-the-world-according-to-illustrators-and-storytellers/

CHAPTER 6

Reflections

Looking for proof—Dreams

People, waiting for something, somebody.

A super highway, separating the land and the sea.

Extra large vehicles zooming by, trees without leaves, sprouting bombs. Finally, the greenest of trees and a bright blue sky.

In our community stretch workshops, the day starts with reflections on the insights of the previous day and dreams of the previous night. The dreams tell us that the day's process continues during sleep and almost everybody is able to recollect their dreams. The dreams best reflect the process. At times we meet our partners in dialogue over the Internet, chat, mails and blogs. Here are some of their dreams:

The Dream Catcher

A male in his 30s, the Dream Catcher has discussed these dreams with the community.

Shadow play: There were three or four pillars and strings connecting consecutive pillars, towards the bottom of each pillar. Over these strings, shadows move as if on a rail. It's like a shadow play using three windows. I am just able to make out the shadow of a horse, a camel and an elephant while it slides from the first pillar to the next.

And while it slides in the next window, between the next two pillars, the three shadows are out of focus and zoomed in so big that I cannot make out the figures. But while they slide slowly in the last window the figures are very clear and sharp.

Cracked: I am inside a maximum security prison in a small house, but I come out of that house. I have figured out how to unlock all locks and doors. No prison can hold me any more. Now happy and enlightened, I am out and I provoke my mother: "Mummy, tell me to go back in and I will be out in a jiffy." Afraid that she will not see me again, she persuades me to stop playing games. But now I love to play it. So I jump back into the prison in the house through an opening in the roof and quickly pick the first prison door with some splinter. The next door lock is trickier, this requires some lateral thinking and so I tilt my head to solve the problem and break open the door. The third lock is purely at some higher level. I focus and recite something and I am out again! Free and happy!

Self-centred: Something has attacked the city and is killing the inhabitants . . . like an epidemic or genocide. I was busy escaping when the 'movie' of the dream is re-wound to the point where I am in a multiplex just before the cataclysm. I see a sweet looking toddler at the ticket counter and my train of thought goes this way:

'Why don't I save the child from the impending horrible death?'

'But if it is impending, what can I do about it? You can't save everyone in this world?'

'You are wasting precious time . . . SAVE the child!'

'Why should I change anybody's destiny even if this was possible?'

Jupiter in action: A huge anantha shesha (serpent) statue is being completed. And in its shade, a commanding looking Vishnu is being made. Here Vishnu is not in the reclining posture but takes the upright one. Vishnu's normally pleasant and peaceful face is demonic as an Asura's (Rahu?) can be. He has a tough commanding posture as if he is about to put a whole army into action.

A lot of veneration, funding and decoration go into the making of the statue. Gold coins are stuck all across the floor. Photographers light up the place with their flashes.

Lost search: I am cruising on a short, black tri-wheeler mo-bike through the alleys. Instead of the ordinary dials on it there is a GPS panel which indicates the path I should navigate in order to 'locate' a lost item. Having found something, I go home as the vehicle brought me close to my house.

The house has only a square hall; walls are all reddish-purple in colour. There is my mother and also others in the family and some guests whom I don't know. There is a mother and her daughters. Too many females in the room, I think and I feel uncomfortable. I go out and continue my search.

The vehicle moves, but the panel displays that the moon is quickly covered by thick clouds and so the search cannot continue. Moreover the display goes off as the battery charge is out. So I push the bike around the house hoping that its dynamo will trigger it on. Some of the ladies in the house ask me what I am doing while they walk around the house in the opposite direction. I ignore them and carry on. What am I searching for?

I go back into the house. Mom asks me something about passport and identity verification. I question her back angrily 'WHAT?' She then clearly says that the 'authorities' need to see facial hair on me to prove my identity! Embarrassed.

Rooting: I am at my uncle's well-kept house. I am surprised that it is not in Kerala, but in Kuwait and that too right next to the awesome Kuwait (trio) towers. The house is not very large, but is well kept and furnished as a typical central governmental employee's home is. I notice that the house plan is like a narrow rectangle in alignment with the neighbouring towers. The long house opposite lies over a very small rock mound.

I stand in their garden, which is well stocked with potted plants by the numerous helpers they have. While this is being done, I have a look at the smallest of the towers in front. I notice that this tower doesn't look original and is smaller than I thought. I shift my head and find there is another bigger trio of towers being constructed. I shift my head again and see the original and awesomely high towers.

Both my cousins are inside the house. The eldest tells me that he has some dental work to be done and asks me to show him my tooth fillings. I am hesitant and grind my teeth in preparation to show him, feeling like I am going to blow off my teeth. While I do this he undresses and stands in front of me shamelessly and innocently, as we were when we were kids. His naked body is as ugly as mine, now that he has a huge potbelly just like my grandfather.

He asks me to open my mouth and he sees the fillings, the silvery-metallic and the tooth-coloured caps.

Embarrassed: The hotel lobby was posh and well lit. Good, light brown woodwork and stainless steel. A short metro carriage runs through this place carrying executives. I am well dressed in a charcoal colour suit with a matching tie and black shoes. I am fitted out to charm any crowd. But I forget where I've left my briefcase and laptop. I stop the metro and tell them that I need to check for my bag in their glass bag carriage. I find all sorts of bags except mine. I doubt whether I have brought it with me to this country at all. Mr nice guy that I am, I don't like to keep others waiting. I let the metro move which moves quickly and is almost out of sight when I realise that one of my expensive shoes is missing! I must have left it in the cabin while looking for the bag and the metro has left.

Oh! God! What am I going to do now? How will I face them? I will look like a fool. I have to be ready before the meet. I don't have spares too. I am imperfect.

Exploration: I am with an Iranian friend, someone I met during the Landmark advanced course, in some interesting building. While I try to climb the wall, he runs under me carrying something (treasure?).

Then we are scuba diving. Both of us hold some semi-precious studded, silver pots and we are supposed to pour the blood-like liquid in the pots into a hole in the sea floor. I wonder how this can be done. I see a hole belching out some blood-like liquid too. To my surprise, when I pour into the hole it sucks the contents from the pot and some water around into it neatly, like a vacuum cleaner.

Synchronicity: I browse through Wikipedia to learn about the worst commercial flight accidents ever, specifically the ones that went down in the ocean and if anything went hidden or missing underwater. I see that India has the credit for the longest list of flight accidents in general. The Emperor Kanishka, the Air India flight ended up in the Atlantic; most horrible, I note and see pieces in the dark.

A flight going down in water is just one of my nightmares. Ever since my mom composed her own bed time story of a 'plane going down into the deep sea', ever since I watched a cinema trailer of such an ill-fated flight and the plight of the passengers in it.

Bored of browsing, I walk into the office lobby and notice the breaking news on TV 'Air France flight goes missing'!

Wet and dirty: Friday, 24 Oct 2008—After some cardio-exercise, while I alight from the car for some grocery shopping my wallet drops into a muddy puddle. It was raining cats and dogs and I take some time to fish it out of the puddle. My driver's license, visiting cards, cash and cards are all soaked and speckled with mud.

I get the feeling this is a 'to be continued' situation.

Saturday, 25 Oct 2008—I am in the habit of reading while in the toilet. I place a newly-purchased novel, *The Abyssinian Proof,* very carelessly on top of the geyser outlet tube. While I stand there and think of what to do next, the book falls straight into the blue-coloured, Harpic-stained waters in the commode below. My wife then 'washes' it with the spray, 'disinfects' it with Savlon and blow dries it with the hair dryer.

I wonder what next? Probably me.

Monday, 27 October 2008—We get onto a coracle at the fishing camp. A stinky wave from the rapids splashes on me and I get wet thoroughly, it wets me to my underwear.

Miserable Marius: I watched parts of two films last night. The first one *The Da Vinci Code* and the second, the vampire chronicles, *Queen of the Damned*. Something caught my attention while watching the first. During a chase, the car moves off and the scene pauses at a poster of the play *Les Miserables* on a brick wall. The second movie made me focus on two things, 'Marius' the original vampire and a short violin jugalbandhi. The music was awesome, it sounded Carnatic. I told myself that I will have to browse the net tomorrow on all these focus points.

My convenient amnesia refreshed my RAM on these matters, but I did go to Wikipedia and coincidently I found *Les Miserables* on the home page as a featured link! It seems that was the day in 1985 that the English version of the play opened in London. I went through the link to find that there is a character in this play called Marius.

The Feather Girl

The following dreams are drawn from the dream journal of one of our partners. The dreams relate to the period of her study of FD, across two years, between the ages of 21 and 23.

The flood: The roads, markets and buildings were all flooding with people suffering from cancer, leprosy and other illnesses.

No food, medicines, ambulances, no hospitals, nothing.

She was crying, was afraid that she too would fall ill. She wanted to help people, but she had no idea what to do.

She looks out for help, but everybody is busy. The healthy are busy escaping and the sick are busy mourning, squatting, waiting, helpless and dying.

A flood of potatoes: Potatoes, potatoes and more potatoes. She is astonished at the huge quantity of potatoes lying everywhere.

She keeps walking to her destination with a few scraps to feed the pigeons waiting for her. It strikes her, it is some emergency and curfew will soon be declared. It is important that she delivers the feed to her pigeons in time. She walks fast, faster and then she runs. At the same time she sees two women talking garrulously and denigrating her severely. She listens but does not respond, but keeps on walking and running.

Finally she reaches her destination.

Playing in the mud: She is seven; her hair is long enough for pony tails. Her mother always does it for her. She looks pretty in her white cotton frock with cute yellow polka dots all across. She steps out of her shoes to get inside her playhouse and comes out with one of her prettiest dolls.

She has plenty of them; most of them remain packed, untouched. She was not fond of playing with dolls even at that little age. She enjoyed talking and travelling more than anything.

As far as her eyes could see she, can find only green or brown all around her.

All her toys, playhouse, earthenware—everything's brown and nature all around her green.

Her friend Rahul, the only one she ever made friends with, is beside her. He too looks pale and brown that day. Shaili asks him: "Why Rahul, you don't want to play with me? I will leave if I am bothering you."

He makes no comment. She knows that he is no longer comfortable with her. She feels tense and decides to get the intimacy back. She says cheerfully, "Rahul! Come, let me hug you." He does not respond, but Shaili hugs him.

She is stunned to feel the crudeness in him. She had felt it earlier also.

She is thrilled, but also feels bad and foolish. She wonders, "Do I want anything from him."

"No, nothing," the answer comes from within instantaneously.

She asks herself if Rahul is capable of giving her anything. "No," she answers.

"Then why am I bothered?"

She does not want to lose her one and only friend.

He is being selfish. He suspects that she wants something that he has and she is not worthy enough to get it.

He says, "Shaili, you don't deserve my words; I will not speak to you any more."

For the first time, Shaili feels someone had came close enough to shake her. She is quick to decide not to stoop lower than her self respect.

She stares at Rahul in wonder . . . surprise.

She kisses him, the brown Rahul for the last time, the very last . . . clutches him in her small arms which can barely hold him, kisses him on his chubby cheeks and whispers: "Bye bye forever." She feels the mud on her lips. She wipes it off with her white sleeves. She wipes his cheeks as well. She is surprised to see the mud on the sleeves.

She feels left out, tense and bad, all at the same time. She doesn't know what to do next. She can feel the warm tears on her cheek. She holds him tight and weeps her heart and eyes out.

Jo is passing by. He is surprised to see her in the mud and scolds her: "What are you doing here, you impossible little monster?"

She is distracted. She feels that the brown Rahul was nothing but the mud she is wallowing in.

She looks at Jo and says: "I am sorry, I didn't know . . . by mistake, I was confused if it was someone or a handful of soil."

"That is ok. Let us go home and get cleaned up," Jo says.

"Fine," Shaili replies with a smile.

Just another dream: I am window shopping, looking at groceries. I do not know whether I have to buy them or not. I am just enjoying the hustle and bustle of the market, families with young children, parents buying ice-cream for children. Some who could not afford to spend, are telling the children stories of their childhood—how in their time, life was easier. Now inflation has made life so difficult and so on. I move on.

I pass by a row of garment shops all decorated and filled with beautiful, fancy clothes. I don't like any. Seems I am not interested in this stuff as well. Customers are haggling and I keep observing, as I move past them. Suddenly, I see some wild animal. It's a sort of a horse, but much larger than a horse with brown and white spots on its back and two extremely large horns.

The crowd panics. There is mayhem. I am about to run but then suddenly I realise that running won't help. I feel I am far enough from harm and I stop running. I notice that I am neither panting nor afraid of the creature. I watch the animal without even blinking my eyes.

The animal is moving towards the crowd with a graceful and easy walk. To me it seems like a model's catwalk. It appears that the creature is harmless. It too is watching the whole scene very carefully and asks people: "What happened?"

And suddenly the whole scene disappears. There is a dust storm and everything is invisible. I don't know how I managed to reach home, but I do.

My mom is worried and is closing the windows and asks me to close the windows in my room. My siblings and parents are talking about the creature and the storm. I'm not listening. I am still mesmerised by that graceful walk of the strange creature.

It's another sunny day. We are out with dad on a picnic and I see a carnival. I don't have any clear idea as to what this carnival is all about.

I tell my dad that I will call him after two or three hours, but for now let us part. I am alone, wandering here and there, looking at the old people. There are no children around. What sort of carnival is this? Some are playing games, I could feel the lack of enthusiasm, I decide to go with them, start playing with them and do a running commentary which brings fun and frolic to the game. The organiser comes to me and asks me to anchor the whole event. I accept. As my dad sees me on stage, he calls on my cell, "Monster, you have not eaten your food yet; you will be ill again and then I won't take you to the doctor." I smile and tell him that I will have my meal on time. I will remain here the whole day and I will get home myself. He says, "All right, do well and call me if you have any problems." At the end of the day, the carnival was very successful. All the old people were taking my phone number and I was saving theirs in my phone book. We played a lot of amazing games, very involved, which in real life I never do.

A good dream! I was still smiling when I woke up.

A perfect match: She is at her friend's place. She tells her friend that she has divorced her husband for a long list of reasons, but has now found her perfect match and married him.

She is back home and looking at a huge pile of washed but dry clothes. She is expected to iron, fold and keep them in a stack. She starts doing it when she finds a glove. She puts it on and searches for the other. She is apprehensive but keeps on searching, but does not find it. What she finds do not match. She consoles herself: "Let me iron and fold these clothes 'naturally'. I should get the right match by then."

She is at an optician's shop. She needs an eye check-up and to change the frame of her glasses. She selects a lens with 0.25 lower power than what she needs. She thinks, 'I have to go back to the shop and get the correct glasses.'

At work: She is leading a group of people who keep following her. She stops at some well-furnished workplace and tells everybody to take their places. She is overseeing their work.

When they ask for suggestions, she gives them happily. Everyone is enthused and everything is going fine. A few problems come up in between; she can't remember what kind of problems. She sees that people are worried. They come to her, discuss things and go away.

She is alone, thinking. She sees herself again, out with people. As if in a drama, people turn themselves into her; and in a while, everyone is 'her'.

She can see a lot of faces of herself. She is not scared. But she is surprised at seeing all the various expressions on the faces. Some were satisfied and some were frustrated and a few were trying to improve. Her role was the same.

At times she criticises herself and at other times appreciates herself.

Some of her faces are confident, other faces are diffident.

She at times she cajoles herself and at other times denigrates.

She sees herself struggling, also celebrating success with all her selves.

Everybody was her and then there is the miracle: She is turning into some kind of a large bird.

Old man and woman: The happy old man is sitting on a park bench remembering his good old days. He sees the kite flying in the sky, starts going after it as the line is cut. He wants to catch the kite, starts walking faster, then running. The line is near, he stretches his arms more and more and slowly he starts flying. He is dead but happy.

The old lady is sitting in the garden in front of her house. She sees her grandchildren playing. She remembers her life over the years—her childhood, how she learnt to cook, about her lover and then her ageing. Joy fills her soul. She does not know whether she slept first or dreamt first. She too was dead and happy.

She meets a boy on the beach, not very handsome, wearing a blue jacket; he is quite frustrated. He wants to befriend her for some reason. She says OK and then he tells her everything about himself. She figures out that he has been rejected all through his life. She gives him something in a white handkerchief. He is happy but does not appreciate or value what she gives. He gives it away to the junk dealer. She feels pity for him and takes back her present from the junk dealer.

The trains: The train is quite luxurious and the fare high. Yet she manages to get a ticket.

Beautiful, very lively girls and boys board the train. It runs on a track at the height of a fifty-storey building, something similar to a roller coaster mixed up with a giant wheel. Those who do not manage to hold on to their SELF fall. No harm done, but they are no more in the train. She could hold herself only till the third round and then she falls. She feels bad, but finds herself in the station.

Trains again, many of them of all sorts—old, new, bare, ugly, rusted. The tickets are cheaper this time, she takes one and waits for the train. It's a quiet night, the moon is shining and people around here are dull and mysterious. She sees her train coming to the platform. The colour of the train is black-blue this time. Earlier it was bright yellow. She can see the rust on the handrails to the compartment. She cannot board that contraption. Standing dumb, she watches the train leaving the station and her. She is at peace with herself. She tried to figure out what to do. Before she could figure out anything, someone tells her that in 15 minutes another train will come and she can take that train. When it comes she feels hesitant to board it, but she does. The train is open and looks like a freight car. There are some others sitting near her. She has some small colourful balls, black marbles, a matchbox, three blades and some paper with her. She does not play with them. Others are curious about her possessions. Finally she reaches her destination in the early morning. The sky is cloudy with a dull sun. She feels lost.

Another beautiful train; a unique one, but a bit similar, long, neat, clean and sky-blue in colour. At the station there is a lot of hubbub. People are not as enthusiastic as in the first dream. All of them look well settled, well dressed and 'self-managed'. The train comes in on time and on the right platform. She tries once again to board it, but misses the train.

The situation repeats itself. She is trying to figure out, 'what do I do now'. She does not feel helpless and in no time she figures out what to do. As soon as she takes the decision someone comes near and says, 'hello'. She is on her way to do what she had planned. She tells her plans to her friend and together they discuss how to execute it. They gather the material and start designing a cart, which slowly turns into a high-speed car, not a very elegant one, but small and beautiful. Both of them board the car. The car moves on the same track and consumes very little fuel, as it is running on smooth rails. She mutters to herself "the technology is efficient and effective".

They take some detours. A man tells them that the train stops at a certain station. They head to the station and finally board the train. She hugs her 'friend of hard times' and gets on the train. People are yelling and shouting. There is no space for the others to sit. People are hanging on to handles, but her seat is empty. She sits on the chair like a queen and the train moves, gathers speed. People keep on complaining about the lack of space, facilities and the flies and mosquitoes. She seems to be in a cubicle and everything is fine around her and everything is in plenty. The view outside is pleasing, her surroundings seemed air-conditioned, the breeze is soothing. She can see the river and the mountains through the window by her side. The train keeps running and running, first through the plains and then the hills.

She kills her father and grandfather: She takes her father to the place where she was born. One shot and he is done. She lays him down and before covering him with white sheets she kisses his hands as she used to. She doesn't bother to wipe out the signs like professional killers do. She feels no remorse or guilt and leaves the place.

The next night has more of it waiting for her.

She has gone back to her place of birth and kills her mom's father. She asks her grandpa to write a will, leaving all his property to her. At first he does not agree. She persists, argues and finally convinces him that she is the one, the only one, worthy of it; smart enough to hold on to and take care of his property so that it is not left in ruins.

As soon as he signs the papers, she shoots and he is no more.

Parrot or dove? She finds it hard to decide whether to buy a parrot or a dove.

Her basic instinct is to have doves. Keeping, caring for and loving the doves is natural to her. Nobody knows why, but Jo does.

Jo is with her when the bird seller shows all the beautiful birds. Shaili likes the pigeons too and decides to buy one, but it is getting difficult to make a choice between the parrot and the dove. Jo keeps insisting that she buy a parrot this time, she is not convinced. A parrot is not something she can associate with herself, so she would not buy it, Shaili explains and argues with Jo. "Sweetie, then what is it that you associate with yourself," Jo fires back. "Horse, dove and you," she replies with a lady-like politeness and maturity. Jo smiles, saying "Ok" and buys a parrot for himself says bye, and leaves. Shaili thinks for a moment as to why Jo had wanted her to buy the parrot. She came out of it as the seller asks her what she wants. Finally, she buys two doves and a pigeon.

The doves are gentle, peaceful and beautiful. She loves them and for a long time keeps looking at her three beautiful possessions, mesmerised and fascinated. Shaili always imagined that if she could learn the language of the birds she could learn flying also.

She thinks that it's not because of the weight of their body that men cannot fly but because birds have some secret knowledge of flying, something that only they know. Two hours go by. She is still sitting in her garden.

Jo comes back with the parrot in his hands, seats himself under the same guava tree, beside her. Shaili looks up at him and at her doves and welcomes him with a satisfied smile.

"Shaili, I would like to give you a gift since you are the youngest and the most intelligent friend of mine," he says.

Shaili smiles and winks her curious eyes, and Jo hands his parrot to her. As she says thanks to Jo, the parrot also repeats the words. They laugh and hug. Now Jo looks serious and says: "Look Shaili, this parrot can repeat what you teach it and you have to utilise this skill properly."

"Properly, properly," the parrot repeats.

"Ok, I will see what best I can do with it. Jo, actually I am afraid. Seriously, I don't have any idea what to do with it."

"Don't worry honey, you will find out soon."

"I trust you," Jo answers. The last words put Shaili's mind into some kind of a quest. It is not that Shaili does not understand Jo's messages or what he talked, but it is his specific way of encoding that Shaili likes to decipher. Obviously, she argues about stuff she finds confusing to her and Jo clears all of it with nature-like dexterity and care.

"Hmm . . . Ok, thank you."

"Jo you are a dear friend," and with these words she offers one dove to him. Jo accepts it silently; he is unable to find any words. She looks at him with motherly affection and he responds with child like innocence. He is silent and thoughtful for a long time.

Finally he says: "Thank you my angel girl."

Sleepless nights: Bare feet, pink frock with pretty frills and white lace all around her sleeves.

She looks at the mirror. Beautiful curls are swinging all around making her small brown face more beautiful. Curious eyes, a proud nose, the face shone with audacity and hope, naïve, yet confident.

She is in her study. She closes her books and keeps them away and takes out a tube of glue from the drawer. She crafts two beautiful wings—that balance each other—out of feathers and cheerfully she tries them on.

She feels light without the drag of gravity but feels the resistance. She can also feel the lift coming out of her, her mind, heart and soul.

She lands near the girl, the older Shaili on the balcony, looking pale and haggard.

She places those wings on her very gently and whispers to her the secret of flying, kisses her on both cheeks, less brown and less chubby. The curls are longer. The older Shaili responds by hugging and pampering the younger one. The little one feels the tears on the cheeks of the older one. She wipes those tears away with the sleeve of her favourite pink frock, ignoring the thought that it will become wet with the tears. She embraces her and finally dissolves into her.

No two Shailis anymore!

Shaili takes the wings off her back and holds them softly but firmly in her hands, goes back to her study, places them inside her books and starts studying the chapters 1, 2,3,4,5 . . .

When she wakes up she realises that she has been revising the lessons of her last classes in her dreams. She feels quite confident about those chapters and happy about those wings.

She is again on the same balcony and observing the twinkle, beauty and the calmness of the stars. She is not transformed into the child yet. Jo also is not there. She is wondering "What would have made these stars what they are?"

She wishes that she could fly and reach a star just to find out what is preserved underneath.

All of a sudden, the winds started blowing heavily and all the feathers she collected started flying here and there from where they were preserved safely under the cover of her study table. She panics and runs after them. The wind is so strong that she cannot collect even a single feather and is feeling lost at the loss of her world.

She is standing dumb, carefully watching where the wind is carrying all her feathers. She focuses more and more and to her surprise the wind changes into a whirlpool and all her feathers automatically come all around her, flying with joy. She is not horrified, not pale, calm or patient. She sits there till all the winds come to a stop and the feathers come together all around her. She picks them all up, one by one and notices that the winds have made the feathers more alive.

The same sparkling star steals her attention and the same desire sweeps all over her mind and soul. She leaves the thought at the balcony and goes inside. She sits at her study table, places the feathers back in their place and starts doing her craft work. She cannot give it the shape she wants. She returns to the balcony, sits down on her favourite chair. Frames from her past flash through her eyes. She is 19, then 18, 17, 16, 15, 14 and now she is 13 years. Once again she feels the same joy of being young and naive. This was the time when she was beyond the thoughts of success or failure, when nothing could steal the childlike joy that used to spread all over her face, a period of life when she did not know there was such a word as melancholy.

The 13-year-old or 13-year-young Shaili was playing happily like a fawn in the same room where, on the other side, sat the 21-year-old Shaili without the will or desire to live any more.

Mr Freud, the two doors and the key: There is a huge traffic jam on the main road and Shaili needs to reach another street, adjacent to where she is. She can see a number of houses and a beautiful park all aligned in a row.

Some children are playing happily. She has no clues as to what she is searching for and why she is this way.

She is in a hurry to reach her destination. She does not want to wait for years. The desperation makes her face blank. No one can read her mind. Freud who lives on the same street sees her and calls her from his balcony. She looks upward to face him and tells him what she is up to. Freud thinks for a moment and says that he might be able to help her. He signals her to come inside. She goes in as the main gate is already open. It is the first time that she is in Freud's home. In the living room she sees an old lady who looks pale, alone and yet happy. She wouldn't have been very beautiful when young, she thinks. The old lady gives her a welcoming smile and says that she know her as Freud has already told her about Shaili. The lady offers her some sweet dish made of mangoes and coconut, which Shaili carefully preserves in her pocket.

Freud calls her again from his room on the second floor. She keeps escalating till she sees Freud waving his hand to her. Freud says: "Come on Shaili, let me show you something." Shaili follows him. She is tired of walking and wonders if the house is a maze. Finally they reach a place where she sees two huge doors. Both are equally huge, but one of is unreachable as there are no stairs to it, but the other has stairs.

Shaili looks wishfully and full of fascination at the door which has no connecting stairs. Freud looks at her and says: "Hey, Shaili. I am sorry, I too don't know how to reach and open that door, but I have the key to another door." Shaili looks depressed but then he says: "Look, I will suggest that you go through this door and explore the world, may be that will help you find the key and the way to this door." He offers her the key, which she receives with gratitude. She kisses him and hesitantly opens the door.

She is stunned. She is in a beautiful garden; nature is magnificent to her. She is mesmerised by what she sees. She looks back, to thank Freud again but there is no one around. The disappearance of Freud seems natural to her. There is plenty of water in a pond. She looks down into the water. She is five years old, neat, clean and beautiful, with curls swinging carelessly, framing her face.

Shaili wonders what she should do there. As if in reply, someone answers: "You are here to learn from nature, the source of all learning. There is no better teacher."

She looks at the source with the joy and fearlessness of the baby lighting up her face.

He lifts her up in his hands and says: "Baby you are so light." Shaili takes the feathers out of her pocket and with all the innocence of the baby says: "Because of feathers, Jo."

Right then she names her angel "Jo". They turn in another direction and start towards deep nature.

Wings of gold: Ouch. She is flying with the wings little Shaili offered her in the dream. She is flying above her garden, home and city.

She looks at the sky, passionately. The same bright shining star catches her attention again, probably for the last time. Without thinking, she heads towards the clear sky with the half moon and all the stars. Somehow she knows that it is something that was waiting to happen. She feels joy, satisfaction and a hunger to see more, all at the same time.

She is flying up, no slopes or curves; straight up. Resistance only makes the wings stronger. The thrust is coming out of her. All the happiness and joy shines on her face. She wants to kiss and hug the star that captured her attention for the longest time—more than anything else in the world.

She reaches the star. There is no comparison to whatever she had felt in the past. Yet she cannot feel anything. In between she notices that she has mastered flight. Her beloved is in front of her. She steps forward to embrace him and she moves ahead.

"Oh no! No!" she screams. She never expected this. All this fire . . . inside the star. Oh!

Her skin is burning, her clothes on fire. Her heart is pounding heavily. She thinks she will die of a heart attack, rather than burns. She had never expected that a calm star would be a ball of fire.

Hopelessly, but filled with love of her feathers she looks at her wings for the last time. She is stunned at the sight: All the soft feathers are gone. The bare structure of the wings is visible. She is not feeling any heat. Her skin is all right or, may be, she adapted to the fire. She looks confused but happy.

She doesn't know what to do. But without knowing, she takes that bare structure of the wings from her back, and like an adept she restructures them, removing the faults in her wing structure; the faults she'd thought about while flying to the star

She puts the wing structures on her back again and enjoys the warmth of the place. She notices that her wings are woven with thick gold wires drawn out of the fire. She feels happy but not excited. She focuses on something that is waiting, seeking her attention. She looks beautiful and confident. She flies into another ring of fire without any fear. Feels that the zone is warmer. She adapts herself in no time to the new atmosphere. The process goes on . . . one warmer ring, one more . . .

Then finally she gets out of those rings of fire.

A handsome man is waiting for her and places seven beautiful diamonds on those wings. And then he gives her a bigger diamond of the same kind that Jo had given her once. She holds it close, in her fist.

The man says: "Shaili take off your wings; your time is waiting. Use these wings only when you need them and the same goes for the diamonds. Take care! Bon voyage." She nods gracefully, says 'thank you' and leaves. She does not bother to look back.

A beautiful white horse is waiting for her. She takes a ride and lands safe on her bed rejoined with herself. She is no more an ordinary girl. "I have come a long way," she says, smiling softly at herself and her thoughts.

The lighthouse: She is wandering near her first school. She has not been to the place for so very long. Her friends had told her that the school was transformed into a grand, beautiful building, modern as well. She sees herself just as she used to be when she was in the fifth standard—in the same favourite olive green frock, white socks and the very same white shoes with the two artificial butterflies on it. In a flash she remembers the see-saw and the small and green playground of her school. The see-saw was like a boat where two children sat face-to-face and enjoyed themselves. Shaili had sat on it only once. She could not do it a second time as she was afraid that it would topple and fall over, no one would know and she'd die in oblivion. She dismisses the thought and cheers herself up and moves further on the road that she has never taken. Normally she would have returned home from the swing.

She sees a chemical factory, beakers and jars, chemicals and fumes. She ignores it and moves ahead on her path. She comes across another school. As she walks ahead she is mesmerised by the sight of the beautiful building. She is curious. The steps take her to a fort. The architecture is both modern and ancient, sort of a fusion, made of wine-red and white marble. The childlike wild curiosity leads her to the grand, dark entrance. She steps inside though her heart skips a few beats as she does so. A huge space stretches out in front of her. Some unknown fear washes over her. She trembles suddenly as she hears someone coming towards her. She collects all her courage and keeps standing there, boldly. A healthy young lady, clad in shining silk emerges. Shaili brightens at once; she wishes her 'good evening'. Further, she says: "I want to know what all this is. Where am I? Who are you?" in between she says: "I am Shaili, I live nearby." The lady smiles and tells her everything about the fort and its purpose.

Now, Shaili looks confident and says, "I want to explore this fort please."

The lady offers her hand, which she takes, and they move ahead. The lady tells her that it is a nine-storey building.

Suddenly, a white wing comes down and lands at her feet. She picks it with love and keeps it in her pocket gently, as the lady gives her permission with her eyes.

They start exploring the building from the ground floor. She sees a dim light coming out of that big place; many people are working hard, fast and silent. They are engrossed in their work and did not notice the lamps at their workstations. Actually, everyone had their own candles.

At first she thought 'may be they need to know about switches' but then the lady tells her that they are not interested in more light. They wanted to live in oblivion and do not know if there are any switches. She feels pity and tries to tell a person all about switches, but he does not take notice of her.

Shaili is now on the fourth floor, a real pleasure seeing that world. She feels herself bathed in energy and enthusiasm. She looks at Jo and says: "Hurray, wow what a place. Too amazing to be true! Come on, Jo. Show me everything and introduce me to everyone." The place is beautifully furnished. People are calm and appear to be washed in joy. She sees no lamps, but there is light—more than anywhere else—and she realises it is coming out of a big source of light.

Now it is Jo's turn to speak. Shaili does not like what he says: "Shaili, you have to go back and climb these stairs all by yourself."

Shaili looks puzzled. Jo says that only then will you be permitted to explore this place. "Hmm," says Shaili. She sings a few beautiful lines of a song she'd learnt from her mother. She goes down those stairs and in joy covers them in seconds; the same steps she was terrified of before meeting Jo.

"All right, can we explore this floor now," Shaili asks cheerfully.

A gentle nod and a divine smile is all that comes from Jo.

"Oh Jesus! What a heavenly place, Jo what do you do here," Shaili asks.

Jo says: "I am on the sixth floor, where my workstation is."

Jo talks a lot about the place and the source of light. An unknown joy fills her to the depth of her soul.

The place looked in perfect order. People are vivacious, yet so silent. Shaili can feel the flow of a different energy. She keeps talking to Jo all the way. She talks to almost every person, and this Shaili does herself, as Jo stands aside and aloof. She feels that on this floor there is actually no need for lamps as the people are aglow.

She wants to ask Jo, but dismisses the idea finding it weird. Shaili looks at Jo and thanks him. She wants to move on to the 5th floor. But Jo shows her the plethora of pages he is carrying and says that he is going down to the third floor as he thinks his work might help the people working there. "So you have to explore these floors by yourself." He says there is no need to worry or fear as she will receive help automatically when she needs it. "Bon voyage," he beams at her and smoothly flows down the stairs. She too wishes him a good day and turns towards the stairs to the fifth floor. Without thinking, she starts climbing without much effort and she is on the fifth floor.

The same lady greets her with a difficult question this time. She is puzzled, takes a long time to come up with an answer, but the lady is all smiles when she answers. She smiles that familiar smile and moves out of her way. Her eyes forget to blink for a while. When she finally blinks, she sees people swinging. All of them are swinging without support, in the air. She stands frozen, watching all the swings in fascination. The place is very brightly lit and people look like lighthouses. She rubs her eyes and wishes that Jo were there to confirm that what she is seeing is real and not just another dream.

A young lad comes to her in a flowing motion. Shaili keeps looking, mesmerised, first at the rope and then at the boy. She is sure that she is seeing him for the first time, but still she cannot dismiss the thought of familiarity. She tries hard to remember, but all she can find is the joy and the smile on her face as the boy says hello, offering his hand.

She gives her hand, feeling safe and protected. The satisfaction of being pampered fills her with a new kind of enthusiasm. The lad smiles back as he hands strings to Shaili and asks her to make her own swing. The known fear of swinging sweeps all over her and she stands dumb, not knowing what to do till the lad comes closer and shows her how to do it. She recollects all her courage and does the same.

And yes, she is swinging . . . swinging high . . . swinging higher. She turns to the boy, looks curiously into his eyes and asks, "How did this happen," and keeps on asking herself, trying to see and find out for herself.

Three pebbles: "Hey, Shaili dear, what are you doing here," says Jo as he sees Shaili.

Shaili flings herself at him. She sheds all her fears and years of loneliness; they sit on the stairs.

The lady is amazed at their chemistry as Shaili opens her heart out and Jo listens to her soul speak. She tells him that she is showing the building to this child, and asks if he will help and show the other floors to her by himself.

Jo says, beaming with pride, that Shaili is a hero and will explore the other floors by herself now. The lady is amazed and argues that she is new to the place, but all Jo does is smile. The lady walks away. He seats her on his lap, coddles her and offers her two small pebbles; Shaili places them neatly on her head to realise that the pebbles have turned into diamonds. She hugs Jo, kisses him on the cheek. Jo points to the other. She smiles and kisses him on the other cheek too. He takes out another pebble from his pocket; it is light orange in colour. This time Jo asks her to put it safely in her pocket. She understands what he says.

Jo stands up and gives his hand to Shaili. But she wants to sit with him. Shaili says: "Please Jo sit with me and let us play cheesier." Jo is equally determined. He finally cajoles her, but the deal is that he should to carry her on his back. There is no way she can remain there. Jo is a dear. She can never refuse him.

More: The lady smiles and says "Let them do their work. You come with me; there is a lot to see."

The stairs are not easy; there's a large gap in between and Shaili is afraid that she will slip through. But with the help and encouragement of the lady she manages to make it up.

Here there is some light. Some people have their own lamps, others have lanterns and, to her surprise, some people are cooking food on the lamps.

They are clad in better clothes. She feels a different energy in the environment but is unable to smell the camaraderie and joy of people who indulge in their work seriously. But it is definitely better than the ground floor.

Then, the lady asks another question and satisfied with the answer she puts a kiss on Shaili's forehead and leads her to the second floor.

All the lamps on the second floor are on and people seem relaxed although they are working continuously. They smile at Shaili; she returns a broader one that fills the atmosphere with the lightness of joy.

Shaili talks to them and becomes friends with them. She promises to see them again. The lady repeats the ritual of asking a question and happy with the answer, moves to the third floor with Shaili.

It is a better place; genuine joy is in the air and on peoples' faces. She likes them better, makes friends and likes one person, Fred, as someone very special. Now she's on her way to the fourth floor. The lady is wondering about Shaili. She is very happy for her, but thought the question this time would be difficult for her.

The snake dreams: There is a big snake, green in colour with brown spots on its skin. She could not make out whether it is her friend or whether it wants to kill her. She is in a temple and there are snakes all around.

She's in a pond and the snake is all around her body. She is crying badly and a friend who is a better player, and used to win every game they played together in those days, rushes in to kill the snake. He is elder to her by three years. He shoots to kill the snake. She escapes, or is it that the snake saves her and lets her go. The temple she saw exists in reality; she came to know of it much later. The dream continues till she visits the temple.

She is on the bank of a river and there are snakes everywhere. The same snake is trying to draw her attention, but she is afraid. 'He' wants to shake hands, but she refuses. 'He' does not like this. It seems as if he is angry with her and will kill Shaili. He is after her, but she does not allow herself to be 'caught'. The dreams continue, but she does not befriend the snake. But every time the snake does its best to get rid of her fear. She is afraid of its touch, the venom and death. The day comes when 'he' finally succeeds in getting rid of the fear.

She is no longer afraid.

Over the course of these dreams, the snake transforms from 'it' to 'him', even changing. In one of the dreams it has rather beautiful lips that one might like to kiss. Other features she cannot remember. In another, he develops to a height of 5 feet and 9 inches. The snake has the power to fly which he teaches Shaili; a very different way of flying. They step upwards and the earth does not offer any gravity. They talk in French or Sanskrit and travel to exotic places hand in hand, from an old temple to a cafe in Paris.

She sees them having a drink together, and the snake/man's hand is on her waist. They kiss passionately and she wakes sweating. She is afraid that she has drunk snake venom. The last time she sees him he proposes to her and they are engaged in a long, passionate kiss. Shaili accepts his proposal and does not want to come out of the dream, but eventually she does. She feels like vomiting at the very idea that she is in love with the snake. And then, those dreams never return.

The bath: It is a spacious bathroom in white marble. The white lights give it a miraculously mysterious effect. The mystery is in the satisfaction she feels as she tries to figure out the reason this time.

She shifts her attention to what is going on. She's clad in a white robe, and the bathtub is also white. She notices that the taps are golden. She opens the tap and adroitly places a soap bar. She is unsure if it is a bar of soap—whatever it is, it is transparent, almost white/aqua in colour. When the tub is half filled she closes the tap, takes out that bar and steps out of her robe to get in the tub. She opens another tap which starts making bubbles in the tub. The foam smells of lime. She feels that the water is thick, like whey, and the foam as smooth as butter. She feels a bit uneasy in her conscious mind but in her subconscious she is enjoying it thoroughly. It takes some effort to come out of the tub and she stands under the full, lukewarm shower. The joy and pleasure seem to last for ever. She dries herself, now clad in a maroon robe; she sees her face in the mirror. She realises it is not exactly how she is now; she is older, beautiful and healthy as well. Her face has a radiance and her hair is long but still curly. She examines herself again, with love and dexterity. Then she goes out of the bathroom and lands in what she realises is a bedroom, done in special hues. She notices a painting hanging on the front wall 'The white horses and dove'. She smiles as she sees a man with a baby playing in safety and love on his lap.

The baby is clad in green. She sees herself looking at the man mesmerised at the sight of him and the baby together. His warm, husky voice welcomes her: "Beautiful."

He smiles and stands up, all of 5 feet,10 inches, not very dark and dressed in a professional manner. She notices his tie is her favourite colour and pattern. She sees herself smiling, flirting as he approaches her with the baby in his arms. As soon as he is about to come closer, kiss her or who knows what else he has on his mind, the baby places a hand on his face and covers it with soft kisses. She has a hearty laugh as the baby is quite playful and the man quite helpless. She finally opens her eyes with stretched lips, the joy, a part of her knowing now.

A tech dream:

Part 1

Sonali and Monali are twins from my neighbourhood. The two of them and I are quite attached to each other. I see some autos decorated with the logos of Mozilla Firefox, Internet Explorer, Safari, Chrome and several others that I don't recognise.

The autos clamour to take the twins with them for a ride. The girls are wandering here and there, quite curious to know who will ultimately take them. Finally, the girls make a decision and say that they will go with all of them, one by one.

But there are just a few drivers who understand their language. The girls don't speak clearly and they have their own notations. The drivers are unable to take them on the ride.

Now some others try; a few of them claim that they understand what the twins say, but then they interpret them incorrectly and make serious mistakes. At times they come across a few scary accidents as well, but not much harm happens.

Part 2

I see a plant with tender leaves and beautiful flowers. The flowers are as yellow as gold, the leaves as green as algae. And the plant does not lack moisture, promising a beauty as it grows.

Beside it I see a mirror and my glasses.

I play with the plant, I nurture it and slowly I turn into a plant, better than the one I was playing with; there is no other like me. The plant is 5 feet and 5 inches tall. I wonder whether it wears sports shoes.

Then I look in the mirror. I see a few of my branches heading in the direction which I do not find good. I do not break them; I have the power to absorb my leaves back into my heart. I preserve them safely. Then I put on different glasses and see myself and the world through them.

I analyse what looks different about the world and to what extent. I keep trying, and then I am back to my own glasses and my body as well. I am human or at least I look like one.

Part 3

I am putting make up on my face to go to a party or so I believe. Some friends are around. They help me and they criticise my sense of dressing, my shoes, my hair and so on. I am to choose from three beautiful dresses. The first is a beautiful, red-yellow-green and magenta dress, which looks great, but I do not like at all.

The second is a pale yellow and light green dress with an orange shawl. I try it, but people say it's not smart. They say it's heavy and dull. I hate it, but I am trying all the dresses just to know people's views.

Then, there is my favourite one; white and grey, made of chiffon and cotton. Light and smart, everyone appreciates it. I feel so happy that everyone likes my choice. I pretend that I am just following what they like and then there are accessories to choose from. My options are heavy metal jewellery and tattoos, feathers, some paper jewellery and there are a lot of other things.

I opt for feathers which I promptly stick in my hat. I don't wear them, but, ah, this is a dream. In between some of my friends tell me that if I wear a particular dress or specific accessories I won't be compatible with them, that is, I won't meet their standards and they won't be able to take me with them. I take care of all that and finally, when I get ready, it is in a manner that makes me compatible with everyone. All are happy with me and all of us go to the party.

Geeks, I wonder if the Google homepage flashed before your eyes.

CHAPTER 7

The Future

Now: Ode to 2012

Apocalypse and epiphany

Thus spake the Psychologist

Edwin Landseer Lutyens—Maya

Land SEER!

What did he see?

New Delhi, Old Delhi

Indraprastha and the palace of illusions

Maya, the supreme Architect

Where is the water-SEER?

New Town, Connecti-Cut

New Delhi, Old Delhi

Connect if you can

We can not

All the ports are already connected

Parliament, the palace of illusions

We don't see the 24x7 version

The rape of the planet

Over many millennia

Disconnect, Re-connect

Divakaruni—Draupadi

Where is Divakaruni?

Nirbhaya

Damini (1990)

Damini—Lightning (1993)

The capital of illusions

Corrupted at Source

Kalakoot

Where it is already dried up

Neeraj Kumar!

It is all in the name.

Dikshit, Sheila

Is it OK?

Cosmetics, Content

Water, wine

Christ, Krishna

Water, Pepsi

Indra Nooyi!

The glass ceiling

Broken!

Kalakoot, Kaliya

Vishnu, Amrit

Adam, Nancy

Adam, Eve

The sleepless serpent

Krishna and Kaliya

Connect if you can

Connecti-cut

Connect

We cannot

We are already connected

Firing on all cylinders

Mad rush to where no one deserves to go

Connected

To the flat world—'Fried Man'

To the pyramid—Prahlad

Some of my connections said bye to FB this week

Some to their world for good

The world of Mayans ended long ago

Apocalypse

His story began

Her story?

Nirbhaya

Where hope fails, fear takes over

Connect if you can

Thus spake Zarathustra

Thus spake the man

The little man who dreamt of superman

Eternal recurrence

His story repeats itself

'Thamasoma jyothirgamaya'

Darkness, Light

Sun, Moon

Venus, Mars

Were all in one

In the Mayan calendar

Apples, Oranges

Men, Women

We miss the dusk and dawn

The windows of opportunity

Waiting for the light

Living in darkness

Nirbhaya, fearless

The ordeal lasted 13 days

16-29 December 2012

The world ended for her

For Nancy and Adam

We the perpetrators

Wallowing in our own wretchedness

When the woman takes to the gun

The world is already ended

The Mayans were right

Masters of illusion

For whom the world ended long ago

They live on

As we live in our own maya

Connect, if we can

Where are the men?

Women?

Apples, Oranges

New Delhi, the new palace of illusions

Rape capital of the country

Built by our very own Mayans

Elsewhere it is no better

Maya-ns rule/s

Statistics, a lie?

Where are the psychologists?

Busy building their pyramids

Long live the Pharaohs

Quiet flows the Yamuna

Kaliya rules, at source

The flute is broken

Corrupted at source

At the very source of our own thinking

Do we think?

Connect if we can

Let us not talk sex

It is already ended

We killed it long ago

It takes a little while

To bury the dead

Thus spake the Psychologist

'Fifty-nine per cent of Japanese females between the ages of 16-19 stated that they are totally uninterested in or completely averse to sex'—*The Wall Street Journal*

Sometime in the future, beyond the waves: Reinventing work, technology, community and governance

A musician must make music, an artist must paint, a poet must write if he is to be ultimately at peace with himself. What one can be, one must be, said Abraham Maslow (1908-1970). What India (world) can be it must be, if it has to be at peace with itself. We need to reinvent technology, management and governance in the Indian/global context if we are to be what we must be. We have come to a fork in the road wherein an informed choice is an imperative.

When the tsunami struck the southern coast of India on 26 December 2004, many fishermen on the high seas did not notice what was happening till they returned to the shore. They were awestruck by the devastation, an unpleasant surprise. The recession which is officially recognised as a recession now is something similar. It was in the making long ago. The IT revolution that was driving much of the shine in the country and elsewhere was a similar wave. Many of those who were riding the wave failed to notice the eventual breaking up of the wave. Enron, Fannie Mae, Freddie Mac, Lehman Brothers, Morgan Stanley, Madoff and Satyam should prompt us to reflect and go ahead with renewed vigour, anticipating the future much better than in the past.

What happened after the tsunami was even more tragic. The relief measures were even more disastrous than the disaster itself, another wave which washed away the developmental lessons painfully accumulated over the years, with new dependencies created in the wake of misplaced relief. Much of what we do in the name of bailouts will most likely be creating a similar impact.

The developed countries have been riding a wave for centuries. The emerging markets follow the trend. Since 1991, India has come to be reckoned as one of them. During this phase, the bulk of the talent in the country gravitated to the IT sector at the cost of other equally, or more vital, sectors. Since most of them were riding a wave it was difficult to notice the eventual downturn of the wave and be prepared for the next. The going was good and adrenalin packed. By the time the floodwaters find the level, many will find it difficult to climb down and join the new wave to come, since, in the first place, they were not trained to climb up. We need to learn from the pitfalls that were swept under the carpet during the earlier waves. Only those fishermen who manage the ups and downs reach the shore with the catch, which is also true of farmers, institutions and communities.

The new India was born in 1991. She is over 21 now. As a child who stepped out of the confines of an over-protected joint family, she took a few steps which gave a feel of the world outside. During this adolescence, there has been some ground breaking learning, essential to face the challenges on the new road. We have a National Adolescence Education Programme (NAEP), which recognises the criticality of transcending the learning plateau during adolescence when young people acquire new capacities to face new challenges. A successful resolution is very critical to transformation as an adult. The country now needs to grapple with the issues of adolescence. The learning plateaus are different at different stages of life. Life long learning (LLL) is even more relevant to communities since continual renewal is the key to sustained improvements and performance, which in turn decides life span.

Work is love expressed, said Khalil Gibran. Peter Drucker continued at the forefront of management thought into his late 90s. Many of the corporations 'built to last' did not survive even the first wave that came their way. Most MBAs do not survive one recession. If we have been expressing our love through our work, do we stop loving during a crisis?

There is no better time than a recession to plan for adulthood; beginning today. Historians will call the period 2008-12 'The Great Transition', if we do it right. I would like to believe that the country will do it though many adults do not do it. If we manage to pull it off that will be because of a rare maturity in the current leadership in politics and governance who entered these vocations when both were noble causes to fight for.

Good politicians are better than bad bureaucrats at dealing with recessions since they go through a recession every 4-5 years. Let us not forget that all of them are in their late 50s to 70s. The recession and the terror strikes should remind us of the role of talent in governance, which needs to become fashionable once again. Branding is essential for IT, IITs IIMs and governance. There is a greater relevance for it in primary production, at the 'bottom of the pyramid'. The recession and the terror strikes remind us of the role of good governance and developmental management. The shift needs to happen at the individual and the collective levels so that the paradigm of survival of the unfit changes to survival of the fittest.

Re-Imagining an Indian/global future

Nandan Nilekani's *Imagining India* is his portrait of the emerging India, from the vantage point of one of those who foresaw the future. To be an Indian is to be a global citizen. If there is one country which resembles Noah's ark, that is India. Every species, every religion and every language is represented here in sufficient measure. It has the size and numbers in all dimensions—it is a veritable Noah's ark. It has withstood all the floods in the past and when one digs deep enough, one will find that what has been worth preserving over the course of history is very much alive here. This may not be true of other cultures and communities. Solutions that emerge out of this context will have global relevance in addressing the single most important challenge of development and quality of life, as reflected in the Millennium Development Goals.

More than economics, the demographic dividend is at work behind competitiveness. Whether this dividend turns into a liability or not will depend on how we respond to the challenge of learning and competency development. While we are well aware of the state of our physical infrastructure and the recession might compel us to revisit the issue, we are yet to address the challenges of the people infrastructure which forms the foundation of all other infrastructure. It is only recently that we have begun to see people as resources rather than a problem. The transformational issues involved in leveraging the advantage remain unaddressed. There is extreme urgency to resolve the challenge to ensure that the dividend does not turn out to be a liability.

I used to get a weekly mail from the transition team of Barack Obama when he was President elect of the US. I fail to get a reply from the head of Organisation Development at one of India's 'IT giants' when I send him a mail, just to test the waters. The same is true of the NKC, the National Knowledge Commission.

These are just a few examples of how people and institutions leverage technology. Obviously those who use technology as a lever will continue to move the world. For technology to be leveraged, the people behind the lever need to be in alignment with technology. To cite another example, much before the security agencies began deciphering the GPS, the 'illiterate' fishermen on the southern coast of India started using the GPS. The same was true of mobile phones too. Let us also remind ourselves that IT did not save us from the recession, which is but a limitation of how we use technology which has by and large come to be understood as IT by our graduates in technology and the mainstream. Captains of Indian industry with Ivy League MBAs who have the wherewithal to access the best technology or management globally have more faith in their astrologers—an obsolete technology which did not do the country any good for over 2,000 years—than in these disciplines. Most engineers too have more faith in the astrologer than in their own designs. In general, we have more faith in default than in design. Even when there is a design and strategy, we would like to say "I have been lucky to be successful." Design is still an infant discipline in the country and ambivalence rather than strategy appears to be a cultural handicap.

The human resource function became synonymous with recruitment, and in a recession redefined as retrenchment or pink slips; and development came to be understood as software development. Till now an Infosys or TCS could afford the luxury of learning and competency development, stretching over years, that would transform raw graduates to billable resources. The gates are now likely to remain closed to over 300,000 engineering graduates, most of whom spent 4 years and over Rs 7 lakh in loans to earn an engineering degree without any assurance that they are employable—the ability to obtain and retain employment when the same is challenged during a recession. In place of the housing sub-prime we are likely to have a sub-prime in educational loans, though this may not be significant enough to cause similar repercussions.

We have a system where the brilliance of the IITs and IIMs is outwitted by successful coaching shops that sprouted and established themselves as more successful business models than the IITs and IIMs, without the huge investments needed to create such institutions. Most often, learning and competency development, the core of HR, came to be addressed at a very cosmetic level with theories and models of building the pyramid without a theory about the brick, the basic building unit. The function went through an inversion as reflected in the coinage of terms like 'hard skills' for 'soft skills' and vice versa, sweeping aside Moore's law and the imperatives that follow from it.

People who rode to iconic status on the upswing, who had never survived a downturn, came to don the hats of venture capitalists, mentors and management consultants. Management consultants downgraded themselves to client interfacing for IT services, and software service providers attempted to reinvent themselves as management consultants. Consultants talked about people process maturity in their 30s even before facing their own mid-life crisis. The shelf life of most managers came to be established at around 15 years, quite unlike a good professional who is governed by a code of conduct and practices his discipline for life. People who designed product obsolescence and product and organisational positioning could not walk their own talk. Graduates of 'professional' courses could not answer the question: What is it to be a professional? The cosmetic was taken care of, but the content was not.

Finance capital>Human capital >Community capital

Settled agriculture, followed by industrialisation and the ICT revolution were the prominent waves in history, which lasted for around 10,000, 500 and 50 years respectively. The fishermen and tribal communities, the ecosystem people, belong to an earlier phase. They live on community or common property resources and have been pushed to the boundaries of 'modern society' which failed to recognise their silent, but essential role as guardians of the ecosystem against conventional norms of ROI. Most of the fish we consume flows from the ecosystem people, milk from the farmers, bottled water from industry and the software that keeps me connected from a proto-knowledge community which has emerged out of the last wave. That fish and milk are relatively cheaper than bottled water sums up the accumulated distortions in the system. While the meltdown continues, Ivy League b-schools discuss 'If you are smart, why aren't you rich?' and 'How to build a professional image' as if money is the only measure of intelligence and a professional image is more important than being a true professional. We don't need a lot of proof of the degree of professionalism of the 'smart managers' who bothered more about their bonuses than the safety of the ships they were in charge of.

As the product is in the process, it is time to revisit the b-schools and the process through which managers are churned out. I pay $50, the equivalent of a month's income at the 'bottom of the pyramid', for a best seller by an author who has been thrice on the *New York Times* best seller list. The book, on the application of systems thinking in an area of my interest, reveals that the author's understanding of the discipline is equivalent to that of a physicist who has only two dimensions to deal with physical reality. He is smart and he will be rich, but next time I will be wiser.

For two weeks, most of my time was spent dealing with two MNCs—global giants—to get some support for two of my gadgets that have failed. I keep getting calls to find out the quality of my customer service experience from some agency to which the work has been outsourced, while I continued to deal with the agony of not being able to get these gadgets to work. The right arm does not know what the left arm does.

A recession offers a spell of time when we might listen better than when we are riding the waves. The four worlds—the ecosystem people, farming communities, the industrial world and the post-modern knowledge community—need to come together as one, as a single ecosystem, if we are to transition to the next phase of conscious and continual improvement/renewal; an economy of love, maturity and the highest respect for each other.

We now know the limitations of the overemphasis placed on finance capital when the paradigm had already shifted to human capital and now to community capital. Yet most of us are still stuck with the maps of these bygone phases, with obsolete maps and tools for a new generation of problems.

India's demographic dividend is unmatched. The accumulated learning from all three waves needs to be leveraged and aligned for the emergence of a knowledge community to recession—and future-proof against all the waves to come and to transition into a phase of sustained continuous improvement. The metrics need to be against the emergence of global community and achieving the MDG, decline of cross-border conflicts and terrorism in addition to conventional metrics of growth and development.

One success story which demonstrates a very high degree of such integration has been the White Revolution in India, though the learning could not be leveraged any further in other contexts. This is also the time to revisit the white, green, blue and the other 'revolutions' to bring them together into a rainbow of sustainability for the emergence of better 'community'.

The value of a new generation business plunges to insignificance when the last employee in the graveyard shift walks out of the campus. Microsoft or Infosys were founded more on human and community capital, leveraged by technology than on finance capital, by people who saw the emergence of the new wave three decades ago. Those of them who uphold community, the real value differentiator over short term profitability, will ride the next wave in the making. Most of the talent, who joined the tail end of the wave, went in for no other reason than that it was the 'in' thing to do. There is no need to be perturbed by the recession, if we are able to visualise the unmatched opportunity that it offers. This is the time to move up the value chain as well as to address the challenges of employee productivity.

Tools that could address these issues of leapfrogging the downturn could secure the competitive edge that would enable us to ride the next wave. The pink slip holders are an opportunity, not a liability if we realise that with the right tools they can be turned into resources with the least investment of time and resources because they had the benefit of some real, context-specific learning. It is ironic to use the term real learning, as we use the term real economy and toxic assets. A toxic human asset forms the best recruitment ground for terrorists. With an appropriate strategy, tools and methodology, designing a more desirable future becomes feasible.

The ground is getting levelled and it is time to visualise the foundation and the superstructure that will be built. Reality can be sliced in infinite ways. We show miniscule slices of this reality on the post mortem table or on the X, Y axis to the learner on the assumption that she would put them together into a whole. Had the approach been effective, the present reality would be altogether different. We cannot expect that more of the same will lead to a resolution of the crisis. What brought us here will not take us to where we must be.

The imperative is to evolve an integral pedagogy and practice to address these issues against challenges at the bottom, middle and top of the 'pyramid'; a technology for Accelerated Learning and Competency Development (ALCD) for SHP. To the man who only has a hammer in his tool kit, every problem looks like a nail, said Maslow. We certainly need better tools than hammers and screwdrivers in our tool kits.

Year 2065: Creating the future now/remote seeing

At times, on certain roads, we can see ahead as much as we can see behind us. I am over 60 years and can 'see' into my past rather well for 55+ years. Assuming 55 years to be the radius of my mindscape, I can see 55 years into the future too.

Due to prevalent mental models I do not see farther than 2024, life expectancy being 74 years in my context. If I subscribe to this, my planning horizon need be just another 14 years, which in turn would certainly influence my decisions, the prime reason why managers tend to believe in the sprint rather than the marathon.

We believe we can 'see' even much further. If we can see through our DNA, and with our collective mind we can see much much further. Everything about the past is mapped into us in so many different ways and we are as old as the universe. There is something immortal in all of us.

We have been using the following exercise in 'remote seeing' mostly with young MBAs in the age group 22-26 years since 1990; and this is revised every year.

The mental horizons keep on expanding, but what we see hasn't changed much.

The trends became more pronounced. The majority was taking the exit and the new generation, homo novus, was taking over. The flooding started much earlier, but was not recognised by many. The minority could not influence the general flow. They found it more sensible to conserve their energy, certain that time would solve the problem.

The markets were collapsing. Longer life spans and decline in births changed the very character of demand. The seniors influenced the markets much more. Most products and services could not hold on to market share. People found them not giving any more satisfaction; that many of these were just substitutes, products of survival drive distortions and had no basis in reality. The gold and bullion markets had become part of history. The chemicals and fertiliser industry was putting up a stiff fight to stay afloat. The stock markets too were on the brink of collapse due to the upsurge of loosely-held, voluntary business associations of real stakeholders. The cities were facing a crisis, giving way to communes and virtual communities living a life in communion with nature, part of a loose network of similar ones elsewhere. People often shifted residence from one to the other. People in the communes lived a different life in contrast to the majority who failed to grasp the philosophical backdrop behind such lifestyles.

The shift could, now, no more be ignored.

Marriage and family seemed to be the most affected. With adults freed of the long years of responsibility and investment of their time and effort in child rearing, marriage itself lost most of its relevance. People of similar interests seemed to band together into communities of practice for reasons of professional and personal growth. These networks were more like extended families. Life expectancy had crossed the 100-year mark, but people were, surprisingly, in much better health for their age than at any time in the past. The communities were self-sufficient in meeting most of their needs. Products and services were by-products of life rather than ends in themselves. Work, fun, learning and leisure merged to become an indivisible whole, and expertise in various aspects of knowledge accumulated in specific communities. Established religions were giving way to a new spirituality focused on conscious evolutionary growth by design.

It appeared that Homo Sapiens was being overtaken by Homo Novus.

Whether you agree or disagree, the future is influenced now.

We can choose the world that we want to be in.

Homo Novus: Is the species of the future?

Gathering the scattered remnants of humanness, building the Noah's ark of vestigial human qualities

To salvage Homo Sapiens from extinction, the most threatened of all species

Sapiens worshipped the dead, never really buried them fully

Oblivious that they were stuck in the mud

They chanted Buddha and Christ for millennia

Not wanting to go beyond them

Found immense pleasure in wallowing in the mud

Homo erectus never evolved fully

Never really walked erect, mentally or spiritually

Just another of nature's game of dice

Now vanishing in the millennium flood

Killing each other in the name of God and Satan

By-products of ignorance, another gate to learning

Homo novus is the human of the future

To be one or not to be is one's conscious decision

THE CHOICE

Homo novus is androgynous, trisexual

Building islands of sanity in the midst of chaos

Islands of love and connected-ness

Networked beyond borders

Of those who by choice, select the road not travelled,

The Road by Design

Potter at the wheel

The river of life flows forever—renewing itself.

A drop from the ocean has the ocean in it

The body is a drop from the ocean of nature.

We are much more than our physical self.

The spirit clothes the physical, animating it.

Soul, the unifier, is yet to take birth, the second birth, more real than our first birth.

It is both a personal and COLLECTIVE CHOICE for true community to emerge.

The soul is the unifier that bridges the divides within and without, in us, amongst us.

Beyond time, without before or after and as 'old or young' as the universe.

The body, the physical, is just the potter's clay, soul the potter and 'time' the potter's wheel.

Potter fashions the pot in tune with his internal map

If the map is of death we die and if that of illness we become ill

We have programmed our-SELVES to die, to fall ill (what a fall)

Life is anti-death and its only purpose is to defeat death

It is not the food or the medicines but the maps that make the difference

The biology of our belief

What we believe together is the reality we create

If the map is of health, renewal, the river of life, the body regenerates

In the flow of life, wrinkles vanish, skin glows, old cells flow out, new cells flow in.

Re-collecting the body that we had at 25 and improving it further

Perfect health is so natural and our 'efforts' make it unnatural

RE—'COGNISE' the possibility, allowing nature to express itself

Not standing against the flow of life, continual renewal

Eat just for the fun of it, fact is you don't need to (see the blue ocean people)

Eat what brings joy to you, drink what you feel like

For it is the soul that fashions the body

The unifying principle, the glue of life, that connects and binds everything together,

That which re-NEWS continually

"I don't want to achieve immortality through my work. I want to achieve immortality through not dying. I don't want to live on in the hearts of my countrymen. I want to live on in my apartment,"—Woody Allen

Intellectual PROPERTY/POVERTY rights: The chosen few syndrome

Hitler is not dead. He has been renamed Intelligence. Fishermen and the tribal, the ecosystem people, are outliers to the mainstream society. The developing countries and the slumdog billions are outliers to the modern, industrialised, post-industrial society. None of my success stories would pass an IQ test with flying colours, nor would they be reckoned as successes by the prevalent norms of success.

The Roseto mystery challenges mainstream beliefs about health, points out Malcolm Gladwell in *The Outliers*. It is the quality of community among the people of Roseto that contributes to their health. If so, why are we not focusing our attention on successful communities rather than individual successes? The latter need not necessarily take us to the former.

Success in history is equated with aggression. Ashoka's choice of ahimsa over aggression changed the course of history for India. After a very long interlude, the country got into the history books through non-aggression in the struggle for political freedom under Gandhi.

Bill Joy, Bill Gates, Steve Jobs, the 'success stories' of the current generation had many other things going in their favour in addition to above average IQ; advantages of an early start, practice, the time/location factor and opportunities. These are the typical American success stories and when we put them together, we have what we call the 'grand dream' that celebrates the success of the individual rather than quality of the community. What does it do to the collective human dream and the community at large? Has community been improving in sync with our other achievements?

Gladwell certainly debunks some of the popular myths. But the real myth is we attribute a few of the factors to conclude that we have a recipe for success. The investment bankers who took the global community for a ride would have scored very well on a conventional IQ test and many of them would qualify to be in the Mensa club. The notion of the chosen few—that some are more equal than the rest, that some are infallible, that some can save the world—is the grand myth to be debunked. Every prophet is a product of the community in which he lived and to believe that another prophet or a set of prophets will save the world is the grand myth that we have come to believe in. The CEO of an MNC, faculty at an Ivy League college or the supervisor on the shop floor attempts to create and continually reinforce the notion that you are something very special, which has become integral to the motivational tool kit. 'If you are something special, I am something more special and I need to be rewarded more by the community,' seems to be the prevalent logic of being civilised. We have stretched the use of the tool way beyond sustainability.

The problem with metrics such as IQ is that they are blown out of proportion without regard to the limited context in which they remain valid. Most often, we devise very complex filters to establish the superiority of a few to justify that they deserve very special consideration, to establish that they add much greater value than the rest. Abraham Maslow was said to be the second 'most intelligent' person in the world. He said "When the only tool you have is a hammer, it is tempting to treat everything as if it were a nail." IQ is one of those hammers. IQ has evolved over time, as in multiple intelligences—gender intelligence, community intelligence and so on. Nature has given all of us the same potential, but the context varies widely. The Infosys founders or others heading the IT industry in India were born a decade later than the IT stars of the US. The lag of ten years is the price one pays for taking birth in a developing country, ceteris paribus, in a flatter world in our times.

Are the fishermen or the farmers potentially less intelligent than the investment banker? We would like to create such a make-believe which goes into the valuation of their contributions. The same logic works for what we are prepared to part with in the exchange of goods and services. The more myths we create around them, the more we are able to squeeze out of the market. This logic, which has been stretched too far, goes into the making of unreal goods and services, the bulk of the market and the value propositions behind them. The unreal has become more real than the real. There is no 'connect' between the head and the tail. During a recession these disconnects become too obvious. For some time, the tail wags the head and we come to believe in the shadow as the substance.

So is there some merit in apprenticeships, the craftsmen's' guilds, the communities of practice?

When everybody is appropriately selfish and we celebrate it, we don't realise that this is at the cost of community and survival of the species. Where are we stuck now? How much is too much? Does success need to be in terms of market cap? Would Keynes be interested in Robinson Crusoe, who does not produce or sell, though he leaves no ecological footprints, the key to sustainability which is still not part of the metrics of our collective IQ or 'growth'? Are we measuring growth or decay?

Your ideas are not your ideas

"Your children are not your children. They are the sons and daughters of Life's longing for itself. They come through you but not from you. And though they are with you yet they belong not to you,"—Khalil Gibran

Our thoughts are not our own. We gathered them on the way, picked pockets, robbed people of what that they wanted to say, did not or could not. We could pick their minds.

The Wright brothers took us flying and we have a DEBT TO PAY OFF in terms of IPR. They gave expression to a collective longing—Life's longing for itself, our collective longing to take off, fly, and go out into space as expressed in our dreams.

Most of us had dreams of flight when we were children. I still do. Last night I was travelling with Lizzie in our first car. We had a flat and then we were flying together to take a look at how bad the tyre was. The car went on and we kept on with it, flying.

If what we think is not our thinking but the universal mind thinking through us, how do we OWN them, bottle them up, label them and hire an agent to market them.

Some say change is the only constant and let us make a difference, as if all change and all difference are in the right direction. Changelessness too is a constant (values, 'thou shall not kill'). When we do not mean what we say, the intention is good but the effect is bad. More of the semantic swamp but appropriate to create 'IPR and knowledge assets'. Those who walk and talk Kaizen, continuous improvement, surprise us, the 'change masters'. We need to do a global Find/Replace for 'change and difference' with IMPROVEMENT and walk the talk. Real improvements happen because what we pay attention to GROWS.

The words we use reflect the internal software, the deep structure and we don't communicate, connect or improve when the intent and the words are not in alignment. We need a new language of performance and improvement. We have gone to the extent of monetising the value of an additional year of life and medical expenses to make sense if the returns are more than the cost! We need something similar for books, other IP too, that adds to the semantic swamp and contributes to global warming; only if they lead to net improvements should they be published. Most often, they are a rehash of what you already know at the core of your own being which is always connected to the mind of the universe. The rights, if any, should go to Nature—the source of all learning. But for the Web, going by the above logic, this would never have been published.

Charity begets charity. "Guilt lubricates the economic engine and charity is the measure,"—overheard.

The chariot of fire

The Indigo flight was on schedule. He was the last to board and headed straight towards me, a smile on his face.

What a way to meet; twenty years to the day since we'd last met. "I am Raj," he said, offering me his hand.

It is indeed a small world. I couldn't believe my eyes. He almost looked boyish or at the most in his mid 20s. The Raj of my memory was in his 50s; one of those who had challenged everything one believed to be true.

It was 1990 and a workshop was winding up. Participants were visualising their future. Raj, a onetime scientist with NASA, stood up to share his personal vision of the future: "I have worked for over two decades on space travel and somewhere on the way I came to have this vision of translating the logic to my physical self, to convert my Self to a space vehicle and explore the universe. Do you think it feasible or is it my personal madness?"

Raj's personal vision was one trigger; an earlier trigger was meeting the Mother (Mirra Alfassa). "Death is not the only way out. There is another one far more exciting. Death is a normality of our present time. In another time death will be abnormal or accidental. But accidents are not all that accidental when we get to understand how the design works. Only the normal can aspire to be supernormal," she said.

To the true normal

The first step to walking with the gods is to be a true normal. What we consider normal is a false normal.

$$R = \textcircled{s} - \textcircled{a}$$

@ is much more than the symbol of our digital identity. It is the symbol of a return to the tribal, to create the new tribal and re-establishing our identity in the second age of real-time.

Over 10,000 years ago, in the original age of affluence, we lived in real time, gathering and hunting. With settled agriculture, ownership, waiting for the harvest, hoarding and barter, linear time came to be. We lost our innocence, grew up in shame and then came the philosophers and the modern!

We need to detox, empty all the accumulated crap of over 10,000 years. It is a long journey. We can see the future only to the extent that we can see the past. To create the new tribe and community we need to craft a rough cut of the prototype. But there's little in our recent past that gives us even a rudimentary idea of what we seek to achieve.

Herbert Marcuse talked about the 'One dimensional man'. We should perhaps be talking about the four dimensional; about the four fold path, the view that prevailed some 2,500 years ago in linear time. We need to see progress, decay and emergence across time, four aspects of the process that we call progress. Most often, progress has been mistaken for decay. Schopenhauer was 25 when he wrote *On the Fourfold Root of the Principle of Sufficient Reason.* One or four is not the issue. Seeing is the issue. Both saw.

It is, however, not the return of the 'noble savage', but a re-cognition of our roots. If you've been lucky enough to have grown up on the banks of an unpolluted river, you would know how much time it takes to catch enough fish for the day, with your bare hands. The original affluent society enjoyed full employment, had very little need for sophisticated tools and lived in non-time. Everything was in the commons, the equivalent of Wiki in our times. In spite of all the progress, we are once again reduced to gatherers and hunters of a different kind—for safe food, water and information that reinforces our fitness to survive. We are hooked not connected—@ signifies our birth in real time where Wiki is the benchmark for not writing something that is already there or can be accessed through a simple search. It also signifies the death of the philosopher's world that we created with a few lighthouse people as the paradigm and the birth of the new age of affluence.

So do any remnants of the original affluent society exist? Perhaps, in some far corners of the world where the modern is yet to encroach. Not all societies moved to settled agriculture at the same pace. The Malabar coast, present day Kerala, was one such region where the gathering/hunting culture prevailed till the arrival of the Portuguese.

Pushing the tribal and the fisher to the edges is as old as the spicy seduction of the Queen of Sheba by Solomon with spices from *Malai*. Malabar was the first El Dorado for the trader and the seeker, companions on the road and the sea. They came from all parts of the world. It did not take much time from the arrival of the Portuguese for reverse-migration to begin; it continues unabated. The Constantine Church met with the Thomas Church here. The faith that survived on its own merit for a millennium-and-a-half against waves set off by Mahaveera, Buddha, Ashoka and Sankara gave in to the Constantine wave.

It may seem that a lot of history is being compressed into a few lines here. History is story, even science is. When facts are stranger than fiction, fiction sells no more. Story telling becomes story killing. 'His' story is complete only when read with 'her' story. Hyper-text is layered and each reader has the option to branch off at any time with his or her explorations.

Philosophy is a product of affluence, rather an affliction of modernity. Mahaveera and the Buddha were princes who renounced material affluence for the spiritual. Spinoza worked hard to earn a living to philosophise. Our modern versions feed on the commons, but talk in tongues alien to the commons in their journey to be crowned. They will, in time, be reduced to a Wiki-page and when the number of hits falls below some prefixed number, will vanish into digital oblivion.

When space and time come together, history gives in to the new R; the net value between the two opposing flows. It might appear to be insignificant now, but the tectonic plates have begun to shift and the process will gather force as we become free from being hooked to being connected.

Think outside the planet

'Think outside the box' is a cliché that we hear too often. There must be a deeper reason for the persistence of the phrase. At some level it stands for thinking beyond the planet.

The physical

As virtual space expands, we are less stuck with the material. I don't have to move my physical mass to go to the bank or to buy and sell shares or to be in real-time touch with my friend in the valley. Gravity is less of a constraint and achieving take off velocity demands less of an effort in virtual space.

We are stuck with the material-physical, positioned in the physical world. The perfect sheet of rubber transformed into a football has no rubber at its centre. What appears to be normal from this position is the false normal.

"Give me a place to stand on and I will move the Earth." Archimedes saw the problem with our position. In the 2,500-odd years since, we haven't gone beyond the problem.

To move the earth we need to re-position ourselves outside the earth, to a position external to the physical. We are much more than our physical selves.

We see the true normal from this position, similar to the astronauts looking at the planet from space. True progress involves a return to the centre. @ is the symbol of this return and the new journey.

Taking position

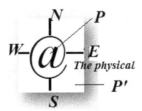

The physical

We understand reality through the tools we use. The compass is replaced by the GPS. We may not care how it works, but we take it for granted that it shows us our position and whether we are on course or not. If we were to develop a GPS for the journey to our true normal—potential—the first step would be to fix our position as the GPS does in our journeys on earth.

What we see depends on where we stand—the position. P' in the graphic is the position arrived at by the GPS and P is the position external to the physical realm. P shows us the true normal and P' the perceived normal. P is in real-time, P' in linear time. P is invariant and P' is variant in time and space. The directions cover virtual and physical space. P' has a time horizon of around 74 years, the current life expectancy in Kerala and most developed countries, whereas P has eternity as its time scale.

So what is it to be human?

"I think the lighthouse people have always liked to use language not understood by the commons. It's just that now there are many more claimants to the crown, spouting Guru sounding stuff which ties in with the term I have co-opted 'veneration of the personality'," says one of the First Discipline tribe. Dream Catcher adds: "Your stuff doesn't make any sense to me."

We still worship the dead. The veneration of the living and the dead are two sides of the same coin. The adult of the species is yet to be born. Our lighthouse people speak to the commons not the academics. As for making sense, this is a long term project which might make sense eventually. They say that tolerance to ambiguity is essential to making sense.

Since 1990 we have been confronting people with the question—what is it to be human. A Google search throws up not one, but 29 answers in the first link that comes up on top of about 1,530,000,000 results (0.40 seconds). Simple questions are the most difficult to answer. None of the answers reduce our uncertainty. They only add to it.

Does more information really help?

Among those 29 answers, this one is central to this dialogue: "The symbol-using (symbol-making, symbol-misusing) animal, inventor of the negative (or moralised by the negative), separated from his natural condition by instruments of his own making, goaded by the spirit of hierarchy (or moved by the sense of order), and rotten with perfection," says Kenneth Burke.

He lived to be 96; for us a measure of his personal intelligence grid.

Burke's 'terministic screen' is "a set of symbols that becomes a kind of screen or grid of intelligibility through which the world makes sense to us." We named it 'the matrix' in our V.1 discussions. For Burke, reality is a clutter of symbols. Things remain the same or even worse in the post-Internet age. The clutter has only amplified. If we are separated from the natural by instruments of our own making, we could just as well make instruments that bring us back to the natural too.

So have we been evolving in our human-ness in the last 10,000 years, since our gathering—hunting days? Yes, in some aspects; for the most, we regressed. We need to put this in perspective as we go along. Taking a common invariant position is the first step.

"Cut the crap, what is THE answer," Ann, another of the First Discipline tribe, demands. We are the only species that can continually improve. We are learning engines with the potential to continually improve on our previous best performance.

CHAPTER 8

FAQs

Why First Discipline?

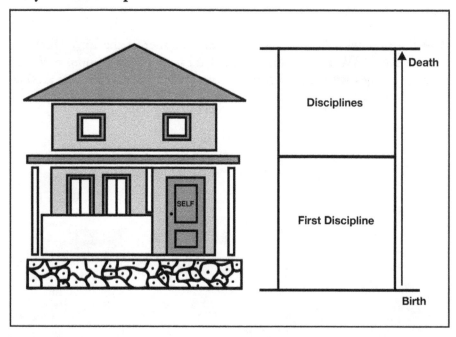

We have too many disciplines and it has become impossible to navigate through the semantic swamp created by these disciplines. So we need a discipline of disciplines.

Learning begins at birth, may be even earlier and lasts till death, LLL; or we die when we stop learning. Learning is the core; the first, and other disciplines can only be secondary.

Self is integral to learning and First Discipline covers self-learning as individuals to organisational and community learning. The concept of self/

identity at these levels and approaches to learn as groups, organisations and community are critical to our common future.

The only real competitive advantage is to learn faster than the competition.

The very survival of the species depends on whether we learn as a single community, as well as diverse, specific local communities without compromising identity and interdependence.

First Discipline is an umbrella term to bring together the concepts, tools and methodologies relevant to this context.

What is the learning outcome of FD?

> Development/Sustained high performance.

Development is the process by which we realise our personal and collective potential, conserving and enhancing our commons to produce sustainable and justly distributed improvements in our quality of life consistent with our own aspirations.

It sounds a lot like David C. Korten.

Yes, almost; except that we are not external to the process. I also learnt it from experience while working with artisanal fishermen for over two decades.

Why did you go to two b-schools?

I went to those two schools as a student to learn whether they mean business or not. Now we frequent b-schools as part of our work. We believe that it is business that makes or mars development.

What was the best learning from the b-schools?

That they don't mean business or they only mean business, depending on how you define the term. This was the best learning, which took us to the new curriculum.

You also worked closely with governments for over three decades. Did you learn something?

Yes, primarily how not to manage. That governance will always be done by businesses directly or indirectly.

What is the process you follow to facilitate learning?

We offer a nano MBA on a one to one basis. We also offer short organisational workshops of 3-5 days and seminars designed to meet specific requirements. Other than the tool and methodology, everything else varies with each student/client to meet his /her/their learning requirements.

Tell us something about the tool

It is a meta map, a map of all maps. We work with you to understand this map and customise it to your requirements.

What about the methodology?

We have a large inventory of tools and techniques. Some of them are story telling, dream design, activities, games, projects, dialogues, action learning and so on

Who can join?

Anyone whose business is REAL, sustained high performance/improvements.

Any age preferences?

The older, the better.

Do you award degrees, certificates, diplomas?

None whatsoever!

Why should I join?

No reasons whatsoever other than if you want sustained high performance/ improvements and to live a life by design rather than default.

What are sustained high performance competencies?

1. Positioning position, Positions, Variant, invariant positions

2. Directioning, direction, True north

3. Reflecting, Paying attention to real improvements

4. Personal mastery

5. System/s thinking

6. Community intelligence, Intelligences, Multiple intelligences, Gender, Community intelligence, Natural intelligence

7. Accelerated learning, stretch—physical, mental, spiritual

8. Continual renewal, Radical renewal, Regeneration therapy

9. Mental maps. Models, Maps, Meta maps

10. Aligning with the unknown, Intuition

In short the practice of three imperatives and six perfections

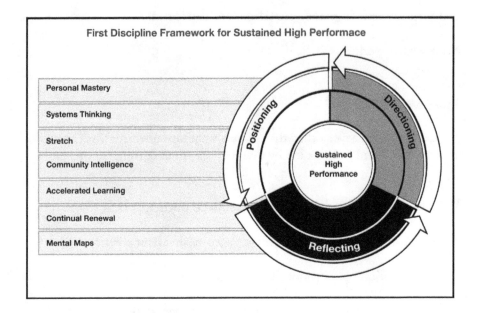

What does it cost me?

Nothing, other than your time. Real learning has zero costs. This is the only real investment that invariably gives you the highest returns. We guarantee that the benefits far outweigh the cost of time and money.

Are there any scholarships?

Yes. You need pay only a small part of the incremental returns that come to you and as decided by you just to meet our very minimal overheads, when you can afford to pay.

How long have you been doing this?

Since 1990.

Do you have case studies of successful alumni?

We have only had successes.

Give us some examples

I refuse. You might meet some of them and it is up to them to divulge.

Less FAQs

What is the first step to a journey, physical, virtual or the journey of life; the second step and then the third? What differentiates the human from the animal?

What is our most basic need, even more basic than the physiological? Guess what? Over a period of two decades, we are yet to get the right answer at the first try from groups of some very intelligent people and their gurus!